Aeschylus

ORESTEIA

a new adaptation by Robert Icke

OBERON BOOKS
LONDON

WWW.OBERONBOOKS.COM

First published in 2015 by Oberon Books Ltd
521 Caledonian Road, London N7 9RH
Tel: +44 (0) 20 7607 3637 / Fax: +44 (0) 20 7607 3629
e-mail: info@oberonbooks.com
www.oberonbooks.com

A catalogue record for this book is available from the British
Library.

PB ISBN: 978-1-78319-900-6
E ISBN: 978-1-78319-902-0

Cover design by James Illman

Printed, bound and converted
by CPI Group (UK) Ltd, Croydon, CR0 4YY.

Visit www.oberonbooks.com to read more about all our books
and to buy them. You will also find features, author interviews and
news of any author events, and you can sign up for e-newsletters
so that you're always first to hear about our new releases.

Acknowledgements

I am indebted to a whole host of generous people
who read drafts, watched run-throughs, commented,
interrogated, supported, and generally suggested ways
to make things better. First and foremost: the company
of the first production; the actors who participated in
various development readings; and, in alphabetical
order, Anthony Almeida, Liz Eddy, Simon Goldhill,
Rupert Goold, Robin Grey, Rebecca Hill, Dan Hutton,
Zoe Johnson, Duncan Macmillan, Ben Power,
Duška Radosavljević, Daniel Raggett, Moses Rose,
Zara Tempest-Walters and Anne Washburn.
Thank you all.

Introduction

What was Greek tragedy for? What was its function in the society in which it first developed?

One fundamental answer to these questions is that tragedy rewrote the inherited myths of ancient Athens for the new democratic city – and performed them before the assembled citizens. Tragic drama produced a new and challenging repertoire of stories for the city to explore what civic life now meant.

By the fifth century B.C.E., the era when all our surviving tragedies were written and produced in Athens, the poems of Homer had been sung for three hundred years across all of Greece. The Iliad, the Odyssey and the other tales of the sack of Troy and the return of the Greek heroes, provided the foundation of the history of Greece and, above all, the images and stories by which people made sense of the world. It was Homer that was taught throughout schools, Homer that was sung at festivals, Homer that was learnt off by heart by keen culture buffs as well as by professional performers, Homer who was quoted as The Authority. Homer made up the furniture of the Greek mind.

The first word of Homer's Odyssey is 'andra', 'man', and since antiquity this great epic has been seen not just as the adventures of one tricky man, Odysseus on his way home from Troy, but also as an exploration of what it is to be a male adult in society. It offers a vivid and engaging story of what it means to care for a family, to struggle for a home, to find a place as a man among other men. In this epic, the story of Orestes is told more than eleven times. Again and again, it repeats the tale of how Agamemnon came home and was murdered by the usurper, Aegisthus, and how Agamemnon's son, Orestes, then killed Aegisthus and took back control of his household. Each time the story is told, it is offered as an example of how things can go wrong in a house – adultery, murder, disorder – and how things can be put right by a young man doing his duty. Telemachus, the son of Odysseus, is told by princes, kings and gods to 'be like Orestes'. Orestes is the exemplary hero for the young man trying to find out what it means to be a man.

Aeschylus' great trilogy, the *Oresteia*, retells this story. It stages the return of Agamemnon, his murder, and the revenge Orestes takes on his murderers. But it tells the story in a new and profoundly troubling way.

First of all, it takes a great silence in Homer and makes it scream. In Homer, Orestes can be a great and exemplary hero for young men to learn about masculine values, because he takes charge of his own house – and because the death of Klytemnestra is barely mentioned. He comes back and kills the usurper, Aegisthus. Klytemnestra in Homer disappears without any description of how she died. In Aeschylus, in the central play of the trilogy, centre stage, mother and son come face to face. Klytemnestra bares her breast and demands pity; Orestes stops dead, and, in the archetypal tragic question, asks in anguish: 'What should I do? Should I respect my mother and not kill her?' What was repressed in Homer, becomes the dramatic turning point of Aeschylus' drama. In the same way, the sacrifice of Iphigenia by her father, Agamemnon, a story not mentioned in Homer but well-known to its fifth-century audience, becomes the trilogy's foundational act of violence. In the *Oresteia*, the exemplary hero has become the exemplary matricide. After Aeschylus, no-one ever again could simply say 'Be like Orestes, my son….'. The paradigm has become a problem.

The new problem, however, also needs a new solution. In Homer the solution to the problems was simple enough: if the household is properly organized with the right man firmly in control everything in society will function smoothly. In Aeschylus' world, this is no longer adequate. The family needs the state. There can be no answer for Orestes until he goes to Athens itself and inaugurates the legal system. Now the democratic city is the framework which makes sense of what it is to be a man.

So the *Oresteia* is a perfect instance of how tragedy rewrites the stories of the past as a story for and as a challenge to the democratic city and its values. What should the city do with a man who has killed his mother or a man who has killed his daughter? What is the place of violence and revenge in society? Can law provide the answer? What does justify violence in a community? How does one family's strife relate to social order? It is no surprise that this masterpiece of theatre has been produced again and again across the world at time of intense social disquiet as a way of publicly exploring the most pressing questions of justice in society.

The fact that Aeschylus himself was redrafting the old and privileged stories to talk directly to new and insistent politics demands that each new version of his masterpiece speaks to its own modern condition, if it is be true to the spirit of Aeschylus. This translation and performance does just that – with immense verve and intellectual brilliance. Take the transition from the second to the third play of the trilogy. At the end of the *Libation Bearers*, Orestes who has killed his mother goes mad and the symptom of his madness is that he – and he alone – can see the Furies of his mother pursuing him. He rushes offstage in despair pursued by these imagined horrors. At the beginning of the third play, however, the Furies not only come onstage and are visible to everyone, but make up the chorus of the drama and speak in the courtroom against Apollo. How can we deal – dramatically or conceptually – with this shift of perceived actuality, where the signs of madness become the real on stage? In this version, the shift itself becomes fully part of the psychological deformations of violence, revenge and remorse. This version recognizes the dynamic of the Aeschylean model and restages it in a powerfully contemporary form.

So, too, the recognition scene where Electra decides Orestes has finally returned home by comparing her foot to a footprint he has left, and her hair to a lock of his hair left on the tomb of their father, has troubled literal minded critics since antiquity – and the great tragic playwright Euripides was already the first to parody it on stage. Here it becomes part of a complex web of feelings, imaginary projections, memories and interfamilial distortions between brother and sister in a profoundly dysfunctional family.

It is central to Aeschylus' play first that Athene establishes the court to decide about his responsibility because it is too great a decision for one person alone to make – an icon of democratic principle – and, second, that the court itself produces a tied vote. Orestes only gets off because of the goddess' casting vote. In Athens, if a trial jury was tied, the defendant was given the benefit of the doubt, and this was known as 'the vote of Athene'. So Aeschylus' play stages the origin of this institution. But it also insists that Orestes' case remains as difficult and as balanced as possible. It resists easy answers. This continuing anguish of difficulty is integral to Aeschylus' dramatic vision. There are very few actions – in the Hollywood sense of action – in the trilogy: Agamemnon comes home and is killed; Orestes takes revenge; the court acquits him. Each play centres around an intensely dramatic moment of staged choice: should Agamemnon step on the carpet or not? Should Orestes kill his mother or not? How will the court vote? Each of these stark choices, however, is surrounded by an ever expanding network of images of imagined consequences and causes, by a swirl of doubts, reading of ambiguous signs, and worries about how communication works too well or fails too dangerously. Aeschylus' world is a very frightening one, where humans are necessarily ignorant, suffering, confused and desperate for elusive clarity. This human condition is tempered but not assuaged by the possibility of living in a democratic city. The trilogy offers at best a cautious collective optimism, mired by the inevitability of individual downfall and despair, seeded by familial transgressions. It is impressive that this version of the trilogy faces this dynamic squarely, and allows the uncertainties and black undertow of Aeschylus' drama to echo through even its celebratory trajectory.

The danger for any work when it becomes a classic is that it remains under aspic, an out-of-date dish admired out of duty. Aeschylus' *Oresteia* is undoubtedly one of the greatest works of western culture, but it needs continual and active re-engagement with its immense potential to make it speak with its true insistence and power. All translators are traitors, but some traitors turn out to be liberators who let us recalibrate what matters, and see the world from a startlingly new perspective.

Professor Simon Goldhill

Simon Goldhill is Professor of Greek at Cambridge University where he is also Director of the Centre of Arts, Social Sciences and Humanities (CRASSH). He has written for many years on Greek tragedy including *Reading Greek Tragedy*, now in its twentieth re-printing, and *Sophocles and the Language of Tragedy* which won the Runciman Prize in 2013. He is a regular broadcaster on radio and television, and has lectured on tragedy all over the world. He was the Consultant Academic on the original production of this adaptation.

A forward slash (/) marks the point of interruption of overlapping dialogue.

A comma on a separate line (,) indicates a pause, a rest, a silence, an upbeat or a lift. Length and intensity are context dependent.

An ellipsis (…) indicates a trailing off.

Two lines printed without space between them and marked as (chorus) should be spoken simultaneously:

> AGAMEMNON: *(Chorus.)* You're getting big!
> IPHIGENIA: *(Chorus.)* You're getting big!

Square brackets [like this] indicates words which are part of the intention of the line but which are **not** spoken aloud.

Double square brackets [[like this]] indicate text which should be updated to reflect the precise date and time of the events in each performance.

A note on productions

This adaptation was written to be staged with a bare minimum of props (other than exhibits: essential to the story) and to be performed on a bare stage. As with any good court case or family occasion, the feeling of ritual is essential. The text assumes that what will be staged is for the most part not the literal action.

In the original production, exhibits and Times of Death were displayed on an LED ticker – and video was used to live relay public-facing scenes. Iphigenia's song was the Beach Boys' *God Only Knows.*

*This text went to press before the production opened
and so may differ slightly from what was performed.*

This adaptation needs simply

A CHORUS OF ACTORS

who move fluidly between roles
with a minimum of costume changes.

In the original production ten actors
played the major roles like this:

CALCHAS

AGAMEMNON / AEGISTHUS

DOCTOR

ORESTES

KLYTEMNESTRA

ELECTRA

MENELAUS

TALTHYBIUS

CASSANDRA / ATHENE

CILISSA

and two child actors played

IPHIGENIA

YOUNG ORESTES

But there are also other ways.

This adaptation was commissioned by and originally produced at the Almeida Theatre, London, where it had its first performance on Friday 29th May, 2015.

The Company

Lorna Brown
Jessica Brown Findlay
Rudi Dharmalingam
Annie Firbank
Joshua Higgott
John Mackay
Luke Thompson
Lia Williams
Angus Wright
Hara Yannas

Amelia Baldock
Eve Benioff Salama
Ilan Galkoff
Cameron Lane
Clara Read
Bobby Smalldridge

Creative Team

Director Robert Icke
Design Hildegard Bechtler
Lighting Natasha Chivers
Sound Tom Gibbons
Video Tim Reid
Casting Julia Horan CDG
Consultant Academic Simon Goldhill
Dramaturg Duška Radosavljević
Assistant Director Anthony Almeida

This adaptation transferred to the Trafalgar Studios, London, where it had its first performance on Saturday 22nd August, 2015. Produced in the West End by The Almeida Theatre, Ambassador Theatre Group, Sonia Freedman Productions, Tulchin Bartner Productions, 1001 Night, Scott M. Delman, Brian Zeilinger / Matt Kidd.

The Company

Lorna Brown
Jessica Brown Findlay
Annie Firbank
Joshua Higgott
Jonathan McGuinness
Oliver Ryan
Luke Thompson
Lia Williams
Angus Wright
Hara Yannas

Children:
Ilan Galkoff
Matt Goldberg
Cameron Lane
Cleopatra Dickens
Dixie Egerickx
Ophelia Standen

Creative Team

Direction/Adaptor Robert Icke
Design Hildegard Bechtler
Lighting Natasha Chivers
Sound Tom Gibbons
Video Tim Reid
Casting Julie Horan CDG
Casting Associate Lotte Hines
Associate Direction Anthony Almeida
Consultant Academic Simon Goldhill

Dramaturg Duška Radosavljević
Costume Supervision Laura Hunt
Sound Associates Sean Ephgrave & Pete Malkin
Lighting Associate Peter Harrison

This appointment occurs in the past

(Outlook calendar error message)

ACT ONE

First, the chorus of actors.

Then, AGAMEMNON and CALCHAS.

CALCHAS   Theous

Zeus. Allah. El.
Jehovah. Janus. Jupiter. Jove.
Elah. 'ilah. Elohim. Ishvara. Ra. Raven.
Dagda. Anguta. Yahweh. Apollo. Olorun.
Chronus. Osiris. Brahman. Buddah. Odin.
The Mountain. The Godhead. The Way.
The Door. The Truth. The Life. The Light.
The Lamb. The Creator. The Maker. The
Supreme Being. The Holy Name. The One.
The King. The Lord. The Judge. The Father.
The All-Knowing, who can never be known.

God. The word was there in the beginning.
And now we're at the end. Or not quite.

It's a buyers' market now. A thousand words
looking at the same thing. And more words,
I'm afraid, than meaning. Not that there
isn't meaning, there is, of course, it's just
extremely hard to come by – with any sort of
certainty.

But you pay your money, you make your
choice.

AGAMEMNON   Sorry, yes, the money – here it is –

CALCHAS   Thank you.

I meant to apologise about the steps, by the
way, it's storey after storey, and it's, uh / hot

AGAMEMNON   hot, yes, no. It's fine.

CALCHAS   This has all happened before. And more
than once. You're desperate that it isn't this,

not now, not to you, it doesn't make sense.
But you're thinking about diagnosis when
your mind should be on cure.

There is a communication and to the best
of my ability it seems reasonably, not
unusually, clear. But you already know that.

CALCHAS closes his eyes. And sneezes.

AGAMEMNON   Bless you.

Opens his eyes.

CALCHAS   That really won't be necessary –

Closes his eyes again. Sneezes again.

It reads as follows:

By his hand alone. The child is the price. Fair
winds.

Opens his eyes.

Which you also knew. But it's your money.
Perhaps there's part of it that isn't clear?

AGAMEMNON   No. Fair winds is / winning the war

CALCHAS   Winning, yes, very likely. Winds, wins:
similar in sound. That's characteristic

AGAMEMNON   Is it reliable?

CALCHAS   You know there's a message. A story. Maybe
that proves it was created, maybe it's just a
story.

AGAMEMNON   It's not [a story], it's a prophecy

CALCHAS   It's a fact. At least, it's going to be a fact.
What you're being told is that the road is
about to split, that an action is coming which
you either perform – or you don't. Make that
judgement.

Forewarned is forearmed. Not forestalled.
There's no armour that protects you from the
future. It comes. You suffer: you learn.

CALCHAS moves to the side of the stage. He'll stay here for the duration of the evening, sometimes involved, sometimes observing. When an exhibit is required, he will with careful deliberation hand it to the necessary person – delivering it into the onstage action.

Two people are talking. We don't know who the man is yet, but we'll find out eventually that his name is ORESTES. Now, he is holding a piece of paper. We're not ever sure who the woman is, but for now, she'll speak after the prefix DOCTOR, which is how she seems initially.

DOCTOR   Just try and tell the truth. Tell me where it started.

ORESTES   I don't remember. I don't remember.

DOCTOR   You will remember something. We just have to begin. Travel back along the road, all the way back to where it began.

In the house, IPHIGENIA enters, wearing a saffron dress, carrying a doll. She takes her shoes off. She whispers to the doll.

What's this? What are you holding?

ORESTES holds out the drawing and we can see it. Two eagles and a hare.

EXHIBIT: DRAWING OF A HARE KILLED BY TWO EAGLES

DOCTOR   What is it?

ORESTES   The hare. The mother hare. She's pregnant with two babies.

DOCTOR   Go on.

ORESTES   Beating in the sky. The eagles. Two eagles cutting down through the air and their wings flapping on top of her and they rip her stomach open. Their claws are hard and her stomach is soft – and she didn't have a chance really. All her inside came out.

DOCTOR   That's good: remember those words. It's a story. The pregnant hare killed by two eagles. And this story is one you keep returning to, again and again, not exactly the same, but – versions of the same thing. I wonder – what does it *mean*?

ORESTES holds his hands out. He doesn't remember.

ORESTES   I don't think I believe in this. In your – practice.

DOCTOR   What is my practice?

They smile at each other.

Let's see if I can understand. The mother and her unborn children are the victims of an attack, an attack from above. Is the mother your mother?

ORESTES   No. Are you my mother?

DOCTOR   No. Any further questions? I'm just trying to understand you.

ORESTES   To *simplify* me. To pack me down into one easy diagnosis. A judgement. He's *this one thing*. Finished.

DOCTOR   I don't think it's ever finished. And I don't think we're one thing. Any of us.

ORESTES   No?

DOCTOR   No. You are yourself. But you are also a part of a family and a country. And a world. And a religion, if that's what you [believe]. You could be a brother and a son and a father all at once. I think we're all several things, even just within our family.

DOCTOR   And?

ORESTES   Sisters.

IPHIGENIA sings a few lines of her song.

ORESTES	That's true.
DOCTOR	Tell me about your family.
IPHIGENIA	Mum! Mum! MUM MUM MUM MUM

ORESTES (YOUNG) enters – played by a child. He's followed by his mother, KLYTEMNESTRA. We're in the family home.

This was by the door. We found this by the door.

EXHIBIT: HANDWRITTEN NOTE, WITH ENVELOPE

ORESTES (Y)	It's addressed to Dad.
IPHIGENIA	Last night we had a dream about a snake that killed a bird.
KLYTEMNESTRA	Right. Was she an evil bird?
IPHIGENIA	I think so.
KLYTEMNESTRA	Then there's nothing to worry about, is there, honey?
IPHIGENIA	This house is too hot. This was by the door.

AGAMEMNON is prepared for his interview. CALCHAS reads the facts; KLYTEMNESTRA hears it like a weather forecast.

CALCHAS	This is the longest period of calm since records began. With no wind at all, nothing recorded anywhere: it's almost uneasy as we're experiencing it at the moment, the atmosphere / staying very, very still.
KLYTEMNESTRA	But how do you *know* tomorrow's weather? You don't.
	I don't want to miss the beginning.

AGAMEMNON is interviewed. The family watch from the house.

AGAMEMNON	I'm in at the very end. Turning up to find it's all over.
QUESTION	So your starting point is ending the war?
AGAMEMNON	Well, I think that's all that's left. It's been a long time, a lot of blood. A lot of men.

KLYTEMNESTRA	Can we CUT the offstage noise please and remember that we are all part of the same family and that to be supportive / might not be entirely
IPHIGENIA	What's going on?
QUESTION	Do you look to history? Do you study other conflicts?
AGAMEMNON	I'm not here to repeat something that happened years ago. I'm not here to follow a pre-ordained plan. I can only make the decisions I can make: regardless of what I say, I can only do, fundamentally, what is in me to do. And that's / bringing this conflict to the right end
QUESTION	And do you blame your predecessors for where we are now?
AGAMEMNON	I try and look forward rather than backward. And we can get so consumed by the local detail, by the right here right now – it's essential to ask the bigger questions. Why are we doing this? What are we trying to do? And what I want to say is this: it's ending. It is ending.
QUESTION	But not yet. You were a controversial choice. An unpopular choice.
AGAMEMNON	Well, look, I'm on trial until such a time as I prove myself. I'm not here for popular. No one votes for what's *popular*: they vote for what they think is right, and what's popular, the thing in the middle, is what they end up with. And it's probably pleasing nobody. Or displeasing them all equally.
KLYTEMNESTRA	Yes. Good. / Yes.
QUESTION	So you know that people disagree –

AGAMEMNON	I respect that. I get the letters from the people who think I'm, uh, evil. And that's fine. They're entitled to think that. But it can't change the way that you lead / and that's
QUESTION	How can that possibly be democratic?
AGAMEMNON	I think that's precisely democratic. I'm not a puppet for the majority view; it's how you persuade the people in the room that your idea is right.
QUESTION	You're not frightened of being direct.
AGAMEMNON	*Everything* is recorded now, written down, dug up, so if you say it, you say it with full awareness it might – it likely will be – taken down as evidence. And we are alive in a time that has mountains of dead words but not enough action. That's a difficult truth, perhaps, but it is a truth.
QUESTION	It's been a difficult year for you, hasn't it? In your personal life?
AGAMEMNON	You're referring to my father, yes? Who died. Of course, that's difficult. Grieving. An easy word. Harder, as we will all find out – harder to do, harder to actually *live* it, to *react* to a, uh, death. But we do.
QUESTION	Your father was also a military man –
AGAMEMNON	Many of our men fought alongside him.
QUESTION	That must be a pressure.
	,
AGAMEMNON	It is and it isn't.
	Look, there are always things we *feel,* that if we allow them to, would threaten to, uh, upset the balance. But you hold that down. It's – it's a state of – the mind is a *civilization*

21

and there's always some army trying to invade. Keeping the guard watchful, that's a *daily* thing, that's a *routine,* for everyone, being aware of the chance of attack –

I'm sorry, do you mind if I take this off?

QUESTION	It's hot, isn't it?

You mentioned your father's death. You're famously a religious man. How does your faith help you day to day?

IPHIGENIA	Today we learned a song for Daddy.
KLYTEMNESTRA	Iphigenia, honey, please
AGAMEMNON	That's a leading question.
IPHIGENIA	Do you want something to eat, mum?

,

Mum?

KLYTEMNESTRA	PLEASE.
AGAMEMNON	I won't discuss my family, that should have been / made clear
QUESTION	I didn't ask you about your family.
AGAMEMNON	No. Famously religious. Honestly? I think most people are still religious in the same way I am.
QUESTION	And what way is that?
AGAMEMNON	I don't *subscribe* to a – I just believe that there's something – bigger than us. An order. A whole other storey above us. And that belief in a higher system isn't a *doctrine*, isn't – a structure of temples and churches – it's – look: I deal in violence: my life is a violent life. Countries run on wars. I'm not a pacifist. But some things are just *right*. The bigger questions, like I said. From there, you make your judgement: from above. It's a way of thinking.

QUESTION	Some would argue it's nothing more than that.
AGAMEMNON	They would. And they can. How do we make difficult decisions? We look above us – in all sorts of ways: to wiser people – to knowledge, to counsel, to conscience. Now perhaps when I pray, when I look *above* myself, people might say, well, I'm only seeking deeper *inside* myself, asking my, uh, subconscious sense of justice – and perhaps I am. But that process of humbling oneself to the idea of a greater wisdom, that questioning process, the faith that there is a *right* – well, any success I've had at anything – is thanks to that.
KLYTEMNESTRA	I don't think I can watch any more. It's done.

The interview is over. In the house, a moment of pause, of reflection, the house during the day. It's hot. The family's old nurse, CILISSA, cleans.

IPHIGENIA	Why do you wear make-up?
KLYTEMNESTRA	Why do you think?
IPHIGENIA	So the bits of your face seem bigger. Like more people can see it.
KLYTEMNESTRA	Sometimes. Sometimes to hide behind.
IPHIGENIA	Like a mask?
KLYTEMNESTRA	Sort of like a mask.
ORESTES (Y)	Where's Electra?
KLYTEMNESTRA	What? – I don't [know] –
IPHIGENIA	When I dance the world gets hotter.

IPHIGENIA sings a few lines of her song.

KLYTEMNESTRA	Could you stop singing for a – ?

,

AGAMEMNON arrives home.

He's here

23

AGAMEMNON   I'm HOME!

The family are together, high-spirited, a welcome home, a family wrestling match, them all falling all over each other.

KLYTEMNESTRA   Someone will get hurt one of these days. And it will be me, innocently looking on –

AGAMEMNON   Iph-i-gen-i-a!

IPHIGENIA runs into the arms of AGAMEMNON who lifts her up, she gives it to AGAMEMNON, they share a little ritual. The dinner bell is rung. CILISSA is there, standing beside the table.

AGAMEMNON   *(Chorus.)* You're getting big!
IPHIGENIA   *(Chorus.)* You're getting big!

The table is set, a family ritual: a white tablecloth is spread, a decanter, glasses. A moment of tenderness between KLYTEMNESTRA and AGAMEMNON.

KLYTEMNESTRA   Hello. You look terrible. Absolutely terrible.

Sit down, sit down, sit down. Everybody's *here /* this is lovely

ORESTES (Y)   Where's Electra?

AGAMEMNON   If she isn't here, she doesn't eat.

KLYTEMNESTRA   Nothing'll spoil if we just / wait a moment

AGAMEMNON   We are not going to wait. We're *hungry, /* aren't we?

KLYTEMNESTRA   God, this thing [tablecloth] is filthy.

AGAMEMNON   Less god, please.

Whose turn is it?

IPHIGENIA raises her hand, another ritual, thanksgiving:

IPHIGENIA   For the food we are about to enjoy, for this day and for the safety of this house, we give thanks.

AGAMEMNON   We give thanks. And what have we got in front of us?

KLYTEMNESTRA	Well, we really shouldn't, but I just thought we might all appreciate something old-fashioned, something comforting. There is also a cake.
AGAMEMNON	Thank you. Something to look forward to.
ORESTES (Y)	So why is it on the table now?
KLYTEMNESTRA	Because the person responsible / doesn't listen to instructions
AGAMEMNON	So we can look forward to having it later
IPHIGENIA	We learned a song / today.
ORESTES (Y)	I love cake.
IPHIGENIA	Dad we learned a / song for you today.
ORESTES (Y)	It's too hot. My head hurts. Why does my head / hurt?

Enter ELECTRA, late. YOUNG ORESTES sneezes.

AGAMEMNON	*(Chorus.)* Bless you
KLYTEMNESTRA	*(Chorus.)* You and your questions.
ORESTES (Y)	Electra's here.
AGAMEMNON	Good evening. What time is it?
ELECTRA	Sorry
	Dad. Sorry. Lost track. Forgot to remember.

YOUNG ORESTES is amused.

KLYTEMNESTRA	Are you a part of this family or not?
ELECTRA	This looks delicious.
KLYTEMNESTRA	In this house, on this day, dinner / is served at
ELECTRA	is served at, yes, I know. I was late. I have apologized. Let's all just move forward.
KLYTEMNESTRA	That is not the way, at this table, *we don't talk like that here.*

AGAMEMNON	This is a time for the whole family to be together, to enjoy the meal that your mother has prepared // and for us to
KLYTEMNESTRA	Thank you, dear
ELECTRA	Dad, it was two minutes late, it was two minutes it's not like the first dinner we've had, it's not important / – God – that / everyone's sitting in position ready for the bell to ring
KLYTEMNESTRA	It is important. It is important.
AGAMEMNON	I don't like that language at this table, I do not like you saying that
ELECTRA	I know that you like everyone to be together. I'm sorry that I ruined that.
AGAMEMNON	And you're missing a very nice meal
KLYTEMNESTRA	*(Chorus.)* Thank you
ORESTES (Y)	*(Chorus.)* It is, the meat's delicious
IPHIGENIA	What is it?
AGAMEMNON	So how was our day today?
IPHIGENIA	What is it?
KLYTEMNESTRA	What?
IPHIGENIA	The meat. What is it?
KLYTEMNESTRA	It's venison.
ORESTES (Y)	*(Chorus.)* It's deer.
ELECTRA	*(Chorus.)* It's deer.
IPHIGENIA	Deer?
AGAMEMNON	Right. What I want to know is – who at the table is going to tell this family the story of / their day?
ORESTES (Y)	*(Chorus.)* Dad
ELECTRA	*(Chorus.)* Dad
IPHIGENIA	*(Chorus.)* Dad

ELECTRA	Not this again.
AGAMEMNON	What have we done?
ELECTRA	*(Chorus.)* Dad, you don't need to know
AGAMEMNON	*(Chorus.)* Dad, you don't need to know
AGAMEMNON	But I'm your father
ELECTRA	*(Chorus.)* You don't need to know
AGAMEMNON	*(Chorus.)* You don't need to know
AGAMEMNON	I know *everything*.
IPHIGENIA	It's not real, is it?

,

AGAMEMNON	What, sweetie?
IPHIGENIA	The deer. It's not a *real* deer.
AGAMEMNON	*(Chorus.)* What do you mean?
KLYTEMNESTRA	*(Chorus.)* No, no, it's not
ELECTRA	It's a real deer.
KLYTEMNESTRA	Orestes, enough.
IPHIGENIA	Like it's a real live deer?
ELECTRA	*(Chorus.)* Yes – well, it's a dead deer
KLYTEMNESTRA	*(Chorus.)* No
KLYTEMNESTRA	Enough.
ORESTES (Y)	It is a dead deer –
KLYTEMNESTRA	It's part of a deer but now it's meat. It's not the same as eating it when it was alive, that would be different.
IPHIGENIA	But it was alive once?

,

KLYTEMNESTRA	Yes.
IPHIGENIA	Why did it die?
ELECTRA	Natural causes
KLYTEMNESTRA	So we could eat it

IPHIGENIA	You mean we *killed* it?
ELECTRA	*(Chorus.)* Yes.
KLYTEMNESTRA	*(Chorus.)* No, no we didn't kill it, someone else killed it
	This doesn't make it better.
KLYTEMNESTRA	Look it's perfectly normal, you've eaten it before
IPHIGENIA	But if we eat animals, animals die.
KLYTEMNESTRA	Yes, honey, but it's – the animal died in order that we all got to live, to eat. If you could ask the animal it'd be glad that its life keeps all of us alive, by feeding us, happy that / we can keep going, and we can eat.
IPHIGENIA	But we could eat something else. I don't like it that they die.
ELECTRA	And you can't ask the animal.
ORESTES (Y)	Don't eat the / meat then
KLYTEMNESTRA	Not eating it won't bring it back to life
AGAMEMNON	And your sister is not at the age to be confronted with the realities of death.
IPHIGENIA	*(Chorus.)* I *am.*
ELECTRA	*(Chorus.)* She is – there's no time / like the present.
KLYTEMNESTRA	In this family we eat what's on our plate. No matter whether we like it. We eat it. We're grateful.
AGAMEMNON	Which is why we say thank you. Each meal.
IPHIGENIA	I didn't think of it as that.
AGAMEMNON	What did you think we were doing?
IPHIGENIA	I / dunno.
ELECTRA	Can I have wine?
KLYTEMNESTRA	I don't approve of children having wine

ELECTRA	Is that a no or a grudging yes?
IPHIGENIA	I don't want to eat the deer.
AGAMEMNON	*(Chorus.)* Iphigenia
KLYTEMNESTRA	*(Chorus.)* Stop. It's *just deer*.
IPHIGENIA	I'm not. I'm not eating it. Animals are people. It's really *sad.*

,

KLYTEMNESTRA motions to IPHIGENIA to stop.

ELECTRA	Dad? What's going on? It's just grapes.
KLYTEMNESTRA	I think it's too early for you to have wine. It's not appropriate.
ELECTRA	It's dinner time
KLYTEMNESTRA	That's not what I meant as you perfectly well know.
ORESTES (Y)	Why is it not appropriate? Dad?

ELECTRA has tried to uncork the wine – her father rescues it.

AGAMEMNON	If you're going to do that, you could at least do it / properly
IPHIGENIA	It's a *sacrifice*
KLYTEMNESTRA	It's a not / up to you
IPHIGENIA	*(Repeats.)* It's a little dead body, it's a little dead body –
ORESTES (Y)	If it's basically just grapes. How can there be a right and a wrong?

AGAMEMNON suddenly loses his temper.

AGAMEMNON	*Dinner is a family thing.* Orestes, before you start, enough of the questions. Iphigenia I'm not having you dictate what happens to everyone. Animals and plants and – have died to feed the members of this family since long before you were around. So. You eat what you can.

ORESTES (Y)   I didn't say / anything.

AGAMEMNON   Orestes, just *take* some *responsibility*.

                   ,

AGAMEMNON knocks over the wine bottle, wine pours onto the tablecloth. KLYTEMNESTRA rescues it.

KLYTEMNESTRA   Could someone – hello? – could someone – ?
                   Fine. Leave it to mother.

ELECTRA   She's mad.

ORESTES (Y)   Why do we pour it into there anyway?

KLYTEMNESTRA   It's just *nicer*.

ORESTES (Y)   Why?

KLYTEMNESTRA   It – matters what things are inside.

AGAMEMNON   We are going to change the subject.

KLYTEMNESTRA   How was today otherwise?

His mind is elsewhere. AGAMEMNON and KLYTEMNESTRA talk in code. The children sense it, nervously; another atmosphere blooms, silent.

                   I thought you spoke very well.

AGAMEMNON   Sorry. Thank you. Today otherwise was
                   tense.

KLYTEMNESTRA   Any sense of when – when it'll start? When
                   you might have to –

AGAMEMNON   No

KLYTEMNESTRA   And we don't know which way the wind is
                   blowing?

AGAMEMNON   What? No – no. Could be at any time.

KLYTEMNESTRA   Well. If it stays like this, and you're with us
                   for longer, that's fine by me. If things stayed
                   like this forever, I'd be happy.

AGAMEMNON   Well, yes, me too, but things won't stay like
                   this – I mean, the feeling is that we need to

move as soon – we have to get there first.
And you heard what I said today, but the big
picture really is we're sitting targets, life as
usual, just waiting for them to really surprise
us. And if we don't, we'll pay / the price

KLYTEMNESTRA   Is that actually / what they're saying now

AGAMEMNON   Anyway. Enough of that. My children, now
how has today been?

,

KLYTEMNESTRA   My day has been busy but perfectly pleasant

,

AGAMEMNON   Come on. I can't be there for your whole lives.
I was there for the whole of the first / part

KLYTEMNESTRA   Some of the first / part

AGAMEMNON   And as you grow up, and this country needs
me more and my days get longer, our little
family is going to be put under pressure. And
I can't always be here, not as much as I'd
like to be, not any more – and I miss you,
sweethearts, even if you do drive me mad. So
tell me the story of everything I'm missing,
bring it back to life, help me to feel like
I'm a part of your lives, that you'll – you'll
remember me when I'm dead and buried

IPHIGENIA   Don't say that

AGAMEMNON   You're *all growing up* and it stabs you from
behind, time, – you don't even feel it
happen. And when it ends, you will look
back on this, this table, our meals, on your
strange old parents and our moments all
together – and these times –

AGAMEMNON suddenly emotional, choked –

it's it's it's – these times –

31

He can't speak. His family look at him aghast. ELECTRA goes to him. Hugs him.

ORESTES again.

ORESTES	There's a dead girl
DOCTOR	Where? Did you dream her?
ORESTES	No, she's real, she was real. I don't sleep. But it's like a dream: it's hazy – in the middle, falling between.
DOCTOR	That's true of most things now. Not quite order, but not chaos – not tyranny, not anarchy, but somewhere between. It's complex but perhaps it's – good. To see both sides. A balance. Why does it have to be only one thing?
ORESTES	It's not a balance. It's a battle. It *can't* ever be a balance. Something has to win.
DOCTOR	And what does she do? The girl? What does she / say?
ORESTES	I'm – this, it's this –

ORESTES holds his hands out, palms turned upward. AGAMEMNON murmurs:

AGAMEMNON	The child is the price.

AGAMEMNON wakes up. KLYTEMNESTRA with him.

KLYTEMNESTRA	You were dreaming. I let you sleep. Sorry.
AGAMEMNON	The water?
KLYTEMNESTRA	Just the bath. Are you alright?

,

He's still disturbed.

AGAMEMNON	Yes. How are you feeling?
KLYTEMNESTRA	Fine.
	What is the child the price for, dare I ask?

AGAMEMNON	It doesn't matter. Dream. What are you thinking?
KLYTEMNESTRA	Nothing.
AGAMEMNON	Was there / crying before?
KLYTEMNESTRA	Crying? Just / Orestes.
AGAMEMNON	Orestes.
KLYTEMNESTRA	He stops. He's asleep now, I think. Come here. Your eyes look tired. Pale. I know there must be things going on. But don't lose faith.
AGAMEMNON	No. I think I'm going to take a bath. Try and – you know
KLYTEMNESTRA	All right. You're in love with that bath.

AGAMEMNON moves to the bathroom, puts on his red dressing gown. KLYTEMNESTRA goes elsewhere in the house.

	Oh. Orestes. Are you eating that cake?
ELECTRA	For gods' sake / you wanted us to eat it
KLYTEMNESTRA	I wasn't berating you, I was pleased – I was pleased. And you know how your father feels about that word.
ELECTRA	Oh. Will you have some?
KLYTEMNESTRA	I will not. Anything I eat in any quantity that tastes of anything and my body just wreaks revenge. We have to hope you don't end up like me.
IPHIGENIA	Is Dad angry with me?
KLYTEMNESTRA	Don't be silly.

'

	Iphigenia? Go and see him. He's just hot and bothered, I expect.

IPHIGENIA remembers the letter. AGAMEMNON prays.

AGAMEMNON	I have always believed in you. I have always loved you and revered you. I have raised

33

my family in reverence and awe of the world
you have created. I honour you and praise
your might and your name and your works.
I know I've failed sometimes, I know I could
have been better, but I was always trying and
I will keep trying. And I ask you tonight: just
let me understand for certain what you want.
Give me wisdom. I don't – I'm not asking for
mercy, I don't want – I trust that you set the
course of the ship. A sign. That's all. I love
my family –

IPHIGENIA runs in with the letter (the first exhibit).

IPHIGENIA   DADDADDADDADDAD

AGAMEMNON   The door is SHUT DO YOU NOT
UNDERSTAND THAT

,

IPHIGENIA   Sorry. Sorry. Sorry – I was just bringing – this
came –

She's upset, drops the envelope, runs.

AGAMEMNON   Iphigenia. Come back. I'm sorry. I didn't
mean –

,

*AGAMEMNON opens the envelope, unfolds the message. He looks
at it dumbly. He sneezes. And then he's violently, suddenly
sick. The note says in red letters: CHILD KILLER.*

*Elsewhere, ORESTES and ELECTRA and KLYTEMNESTRA. CILISSA
cleans.*

ELECTRA   There's going to be a war, isn't there?

KLYTEMNESTRA   There's already a war.

ELECTRA   Do you ever worry he'll – not come back?

,

KLYTEMNESTRA	I do, actually. But there's no point worrying about the future.
ELECTRA	No. It's scary though.
KLYTEMNESTRA	Things don't happen. We make things happen. Your father was told – long before you, before me, even, before we were [married] – that he would die in water. And when he told me that story, do you know what I said to him? It's nonsense. And it is.

In the bathroom, AGAMEMNON turns off the bath taps.

ORESTES (Y)	Will I ever be a mum?
KLYTEMNESTRA	Dad. Will you ever be a dad.
ORESTES (Y)	Dads love girls the most. They do.
ELECTRA	Who tells you how? to be a dad?
KLYTEMNESTRA	You tell yourself. And you ask people bigger than you.
ORESTES (Y)	How does it feel though to be a dad?
KLYTEMNESTRA	Well, I don't [know] – it's a change. When you and your sister were born, I suddenly felt this burning need to stay alive. I am alive, I thought, and now I *can't* die: he needs me to keep living, small soft helpless little thing. And I still feel like that, even when the whole old place is falling apart, and it's too hot, and the systems don't work, and no one knows what to do.
ORESTES (Y)	How do wars end?
KLYTEMNESTRA	I don't know, darling. Someone breaks. Someone wins.
ELECTRA	You don't agree with it. With what he thinks about – going there? About the war?
KLYTEMNESTRA	Not about everything, no.
ELECTRA	Do you love him?

KLYTEMNESTRA	Yes. I really do.

,

ELECTRA	You look nice. By the way.
KLYTEMNESTRA	Thank you, dear.
	The light's going, melting, kind of. Butterscotch. What an evening.

The bathroom. AGAMEMNON has got IPHIGENIA back. There should be a sense throughout the below that he is about to kill her.

IPHIGENIA	Did you lock the door?
AGAMEMNON	Force of habit. Sorry. You can unlock it. Unlock it.
IPHIGENIA	Why are you angry with me?
AGAMEMNON	I'm not angry with you. It's nothing to do with you. Honestly. Come on. Chat to me.
IPHIGENIA	I'm glad that I don't have to go to work. What do you do at work when there isn't a war?
AGAMEMNON	There is a war.
IPHIGENIA	Yes, but you aren't at it.
AGAMEMNON	In one way, I am. I'm – between there and here.
IPHIGENIA	We learned a song today for you. Mum said it was one you liked.
AGAMEMNON	Did you?
IPHIGENIA	Sometimes I worry that maybe one day you'll die. And we'll be sad.
AGAMEMNON	I will, sweetheart.
IPHIGENIA	Not soon, though?
AGAMEMNON	Well, I hope not.

IPHIGENIA   But your job means that's it's more likely,
doesn't it?

AGAMEMNON   Not really.

Are you going to sing this song for me?

IPHIGENIA   I don't want to do it now. Actually no I do
but my body's saying no. You know that
feeling.

AGAMEMNON   I know that feeling.

IPHIGENIA   When there's something you have to do –
but you can't?

AGAMEMNON looks at her. He winds the dressing gown cord around his hands, ready to strangle her.

I should just do it. Get on with it. NOW. DO
IT. DO IT. DO IT.

She has her eyes shut.

,

All right.

IPHIGENIA sings the first verse of her song, and one line of the chorus and then stops. Looks at him.

This is everyone. For everyone.

AGAMEMNON   What?

IPHIGENIA   There's a word for it. The everyone – Can't
remember it. We know it, but …

You don't like it.

,

AGAMEMNON   I love it. It's brilliant. You're brilliant,
sweetheart. Well done.

AGAMEMNON hugs his daughter.

IPHIGENIA   Chorus. That's the word. I knew I knew it.

You don't wash yourself in the bath, anyway,
you just sit there. Don't blame me if you
never get clean.

She leaves. AGAMEMNON reels, inhales. Elsewhere:

KLYTEMNESTRA   My little warrior

ORESTES (Y)   I wasn't

KLYTEMNESTRA   What?

ORESTES (Y)   Worrying.

KLYTEMNESTRA   Warrior, I said, silly, *warrior.* You're not
worried, are you, darling?

ORESTES (Y)   No. It's strange how words sound so much
like each other.

KLYTEMNESTRA   You never stop thinking, do you? Bathtime.

*KLYTEMNESTRA and AGAMEMNON meet as he leaves the bathroom
– and he catches sight of MENELAUS and TALTHYBIUS standing
in the house. MENELAUS is a little younger than AGAMEMNON;
TALTHYBIUS younger than both of them. KLYTEMNESTRA takes
ORESTES and IPHIGENIA into the bathroom and the children
are bathed.*

AGAMEMNON   I didn't know you'd all be standing in the
hall. It's bathtime. Sorry / about the

MENELAUS   I'm sorry to do this so late, but there's been a
development, it / was something you needed
to hear

AGAMEMNON   That's fine, what's happening? I'm sorry it's
so hot in here.

TALTHYBIUS   There is a communication, and it seems
reasonably, not unusually, clear: the
submission is that the enemy is mobilising
– a huge movement of troops into positions
which suggest we are extremely close to an /
attack

AGAMEMNON   So we need to strike first

MENELAUS	Yes.
AGAMEMNON	And that's what you're here to advise me to do?
MENELAUS	Weather conditions are far from ideal / but [no other options now]
AGAMEMNON	Is it – reliable?
TALTHYBIUS	The / message
AGAMEMNON	Prophecy. Communication. Call it what you want, is it reliable as an indication of what is going to happen?
MENELAUS	Agamemnon –
TALTHYBIUS	Yes / we think it is.
AGAMEMNON	So where's your document? What is your recommendation?
TALTHYBIUS	It's a complex / situation.
AGAMEMNON	That is not, that is *not* an answer, I'm sorry but I am so sick of being offered complexity like it's in any way a useful endpoint. This conflict is now *my* prerogative: the buck has stopped. I long for something I can do. Give me *options*. We run the better part of the *world*. Great men have sat in your chairs. Honour their memories.
	It seems pretty *simple* to me.
	,
MENELAUS	Agamemnon, he knows. He knows the – full extent of the situation
	,
AGAMEMNON	You gave your word. He knows about –
MENELAUS	Your daughter. Yes.
AGAMEMNON	You gave your *word* – so what's the counsel, then? Why have you come? Because what

	has been suggested is an unthinkable course of action. I'm not going to do it. So we will need to look at it some other way.
MENELAUS	We're here to try and help / and I gave my word to
AGAMEMNON	And you take it at face value, this – prophecy? You're prepared to have me make a judgement entirely based on faith?
TALTHYBIUS	Are you asking me?
AGAMEMNON	*Yes*
TALTHYBIUS	I think, well, I think you were elected for you to use *your* judgement.
AGAMEMNON	And if it got out – if the public found / out
MENELAUS	Then there could be nothing more fundamental, no greater / sacrifice
AGAMEMNON	They don't all believe what I believe: if it got out, they'd think a fanatic did what fanatics do
MENELAUS	Not when they see the consequences, not when the war is / won
AGAMEMNON	It's acting on *faith, killing* in the hope that there'll be a certain / outcome
MENELAUS	All acting is acting on / faith
AGAMEMNON	But nothing is this certain, not to them. I'd be a fanatic –
MENELAUS	You would be putting this country before your family *in real terms.* Your fear of them is totally absurd. And out of date. This *is* public. This is absolutely about them, about everyone. You'd hold their kids up higher than your own, and – if *that* got out, you would be – idolised. That is by anybody's standards an act of heroism worthy of the highest conceivable honour.

,

AGAMEMNON	So you've come to persuade me to do it.
	Say it isn't true. Let's say I did this, we went ahead, my daughter dies by my hand alone, the child is the price, but then the fair winds just do not blow. Silence. And it turns out we *read it wrong*, that there was some kind of flaw in the plan – and we are still at war
MENELAUS	Then the men know what their sacrifice / is worth
AGAMEMNON	This is not a public / thing
TALTHYBIUS	It would be preferable to – doing nothing, if the prophecy is real
AGAMEMNON	*If* the prophecy is real
MENELAUS	You have had the second opinions, checked and re-checked and it's always exactly the same. I'm saying: I believe the thing and so do you.

,

We brought these. I thought it might help.

EXHIBIT: SEVERAL PORTRAITS OF SOLDIERS

TALTHYBIUS	This is the commanding officer of each unit of / the defence staff, there are over [two hundred men]
AGAMEMNON	I know the men, I know their ranks and their / faces
TALTHYBIUS	But you don't know their families. These faces are brothers and fathers and sons. Almost every one of these is dad. And no one thinks this thing is close to the end. It's cut in deep, it's gone too far for that. And our enemy is prepared, planning *years* beyond –

so there's no road to the end of this / that's
swift

AGAMEMNON   I know. I know

TALTHYBIUS   But if we won. If it was ended, could be
ended: no more deaths. No broken families
following after coffins. No urns packed
smooth with ashes. The thousands of lives
that we'd save if it ended even a year early.
These lives for these families in this army, in
this *country,* never mind the people in the
other camp on the other side of the ocean,
the pure number of lives you would save –

AGAMEMNON   I understand the point. But what I'm being
asked to do – I can't – my brain can't hold it
as an *argument*

MENELAUS   What more could you give than your child?
This sacrifice / would be a monument.

AGAMEMNON   Murder. At least talk to me like a man, don't
give me sacrifice when what you mean / is
[murder]

MENELAUS   It's never been murder before. When the men
die, you never used that word. Their deaths
are in service of a greater cause – they're
heroes, not victims. They made a sacrifice. An
active thing, a decision *they* made.

AGAMEMNON   But they are ugly deaths, unpeaceful deaths,
and she has not made that choice, she is not
a soldier

MENELAUS   But you are.

AGAMEMNON   In no code or system or law – no social law,
even the law of nature, is this considered to –
and I know that there is a higher power and
a bigger picture – but she is not a soldier, for
her to die / like that

MENELAUS   She wouldn't die like that.

AGAMEMNON	It said 'by his hand alone', the prophecy; I think that's pretty clear –
MENELAUS	It is, but – if – if you go ahead
AGAMEMNON	What if I don't? What happens then? If I refuse to 'go ahead'?
MENELAUS	*(Chorus.)* Then they'll [take other measures to insist that you do]
TALTHYBIUS	*(Chorus.)* Then we remain at your command.

,

MENELAUS	But if you go ahead, the means, we'd submit, it's a gentle process. Humane. Preparations have been made / to move forward
AGAMEMNON	Preparations
MENELAUS	Yes. I don't know what you think you gain by hearing me say the words. I know you know we would prepare in case that was the decision you made. And there are plans for both roads forward. You don't need to hear / the details
AGAMEMNON	'By his hand alone'. I *can't* just close my eyes. Go on.
MENELAUS	She wouldn't feel anything.
AGAMEMNON	*Go on.*

CALCHAS reads the facts.

CALCHAS	Administering first orally an ultra-short action compound, active ingredient metoclopramide, at a dose of 70mg, which acts as an antiemetic in order to prevent later vomiting. Then following the removal of any clothing likely to impede blood flow around the chest or upper arms, checks are undertaken to ensure that the procedure is fully understood by the parties before it begins. Following the success of these,

administering a single tablet with active ingredients sodium pentobarbital at 75mg and phenytoin sodium at 30mg. This solution has a particularly bitter taste, so a sweet drink is normally offered thereafter for comfort. Sleep would follow, then unconsciousness. The central nervous system is almost immediately depressed, inhibiting the stimulation of any muscles, followed eventually by respiratory arrest and circulatory collapse, cerebral death and cardiac arrest. No discomfort would be experienced.

AGAMEMNON   And the [body] – she would be unmarked?

CALCHAS   Entirely unmarked.

AGAMEMNON   I wouldn't want her body to be harmed. If we –

CALCHAS   *(Chorus.)* Yes

MENELAUS   *(Chorus.)* Yes, obviously it's not [a given that we go ahead]

TALTHYBIUS   *(Chorus.)* Yes.

AGAMEMNON   Thank you.

And the recommendation is unanimous?

TALTHYBIUS   Yes.

AGAMEMNON   You're not her father.

I didn't ask to be here. / I didn't ask to be in the middle of this complete and utter –

TALTHYBIUS   No.

AGAMEMNON   I should resign.

I am in no way fit to make this judgement. I cannot – I cannot in good conscience make this decision

MENELAUS   Agamemnon –

AGAMEMNON   I've been dreaming, the last nights – the colours inside my mind, it's – like I'm living in a cartoon, a nightmare or something, but I've been wondering if I might be unwell. Mentally.

I should resign. No: the life I should take is my own.

MENELAUS   And if you did, this decision would come in front of council, we'd meet, we'd talk, we'd put it to a vote. And in that room, the room that runs the better part of the world, there's not a man would vote *against* her death. Not him. Not even me. The price of her life, the *cost* is too high. One life to end / the whole sorry

AGAMEMNON   It's just wrong

MENELAUS   But if *she* doesn't feel pain, and it is a civilised procedure, and it is the clear and greater good then / who are the victims

AGAMEMNON   It's just WRONG

MENELAUS   Wrong in the sight of whom?

AGAMEMNON   In the sight of [god] –

,

Give us the room.

And hey – I know, I'm – that's a good night's service.

TALTHYBIUS   I'll wait / outside

AGAMEMNON   It's fine. It's late. Go home.

TALTHYBIUS leaves.

I want to pray. I want to pray.

AGAMEMNON prays.

Father. I ask a second time. I will do what you want. I am your humble servant, we, my brother and I, we bow before your might, and will obey. But let me understand the

45

justice that will follow, let me – let me want
what you want. Let me understand.

,

MENELAUS It isn't death you're afraid to [inflict] – it's
suffering. You don't want her to suffer – and
she won't. She won't *know* her death, she
can't, who does, it's just *absence*.

AGAMEMNON But what she would *lose*: growing up, her hair
longer, her *mind*, her first – love – first taste of
wine, we're taking all of that away, her future

MENELAUS But that's not, we know that's not the world,
I know you know that that's *not true*, it's just
a story you're telling yourself to make this
harder than it / is

AGAMEMNON Harder than it is

MENELAUS Why are you alive? Why do you stay alive?
What do you hope will happen? What
makes it worth another day, the next day,
continuing? What do you want from it?
Because the life you want for her, the quality
of [life] – all of the things you just [said], is not
an option, is not going to happen. We have
not made that world. If she's alive, it does
not look like that. It just doesn't. It wouldn't
look like *this*. We lose the war. We're defeated.
Dominated. Slaves, and prisoners – and
worse. She's a beautiful girl. Imagine her.
In that world. And if you think that, of all
people, your family would have any chance,
any chance at all, of staying in this house –
that *she* would have any chance of *anything* –

Even to us. Our people. She would be alive,
the fact of *her being alive,* would be instead of
their daughters and their brothers, pits full of
corpses that didn't need to die. The weight of
that brought down on them because of her.

	They'd curse her name. That's not a world in which she'd want to live. She *only* suffers if she stays alive.
AGAMEMNON	She is a child. Just / a child.
MENELAUS	But you can see her future. And unlike every other parent, you're not pushing her forwards into a world you've failed to guarantee. You *know* there's nothing good to come. She only suffers if she stays alive.

,

AGAMEMNON	I worshipped them when I was young – the generals, their ranks, their battles, their medals, you know? They moved the borders of the world. They were *huge*. And then somehow, their names became our names – those bronze-edged portraits were *of us* – and you realise that you're now sitting in their seats, the holder of their offices – and it's so *disappointing*. It's not heroic, you're not making history: just compromising, problem-solving, hoping against hope that something can at some point be achieved – day to day to day. It's just *people*.
MENELAUS	And that wouldn't be different for her. She'd just become an adult. Like me. Flawed and sweaty and fundamentally sad.
	But it is different for you. You're my brother, Agamemnon but – it is different for you – because I think you're about to do something that will unlock every thing else, something that makes you a thousand times any of the people who came before you. You – and her. An act of sacrifice that will – actually make things better. And god knows, god knows that on a thousand fronts we need that now.

,

AGAMEMNON	I don't want it to be public. We cover it up. We bury it down so deep that no one ever finds out.
AGAMEMNON	*(Chorus.)* All right?
MENELAUS	*(Chorus.)* All right.

AGAMEMNON sort of laughs.

AGAMEMNON	Look at us. Given the man Dad was, given what happened, you have to think that we managed to drag the family line forward a certain distance. Considering how it was in this house, how we could have just been eaten up by all of it. And if we manage to do one thing that's good, in its own way that's astonishing.

MENELAUS laughs too.

	I don't know why I'm laughing. It's just sort of coming out.
	It's important that she – she doesn't *speak,* can't – during
MENELAUS	Yes. She won't feel anything. I promise you that. And we'll give you all, the whole family something to ensure you sleep. During.
AGAMEMNON	And in the morning, we wake up, she finds her daughter in bed
MENELAUS	Natural causes. You won't see anything.
AGAMEMNON	That isn't what it says. It's 'by my hand', not 'by my order': it has to be me. It's my judgement – it's right I should be there.
MENELAUS	I'll be right next to you. I'll – come back later to – but I need to go, to arrange [everything] – I want to say I'm proud / of you
AGAMEMNON	I just don't understand what this is *for.*
MENELAUS	It's the right thing. It is an impossible decision

AGAMEMNON hears this afresh.

AGAMEMNON   It is not a decision, she is my daughter.
Can you just. She is your niece, she is my
daughter, and as her *family*, we – for crying
out *loud* it's not something I am doing *lightly*
SHE IS MY FUCKING DAUGHTER.

I'm sorry, I'm – can you stay for –

But MENELAUS is gone.

                    ,

KLYTEMNESTRA and AGAMEMNON.

Oh. Hello. I didn't think you'd be up

KLYTEMNESTRA   You didn't think I'd be up

What you said to me before. I just … this is
going to sound silly, 'The child is the price.'
I know it's [secret], you can't discuss it, but I
just – I'm just saying, be careful. If people's
children are involved. I know your tracks are
covered and it's in service of the country, but
it comes back to you if it's your decision, and
if someone found out – the cost to us, to all
of us

AGAMEMNON   You're all well protected

KLYTEMNESTRA   What's wrong? What's wrong?

AGAMEMNON   I'm just – too hot. There's – no, I'm – just

*He suddenly, forcefully tries to kiss her. She, surprised, stops
him – then:*

KLYTEMNESTRA   Promise me – I'm saying, if I've read it right,
'the child is the price' – promise me you
won't get hurt

AGAMEMNON   I won't. / We won't

KLYTEMNESTRA   Agamemnon / I worry

AGAMEMNON   No revenge. No chance of that.

KLYTEMNESTRA   How can you be sure?

AGAMEMNON   I'm sure. *I'm sure.* I really don't want to keep talking about this, Klytemnestra, I really don't.

,

KLYTEMNESTRA   It was a dream. Why are you – ?

,

'The child is the price'. It's. It's our child.

That's what it meant.

You can't think that you're going to [do it]. I don't believe that there's even a world in which you could consider – I can't – believe this, I can't believe / you

AGAMEMNON   I was going to tell you, Klytemnestra, listen –

KLYTEMNESTRA   It was a dream. A *dream.*

AGAMEMNON   It's more than that. I need you to listen to me. I'll tell you the truth, but I need you to understand. Please. *Everything* is telling me that something *more* is happening here, there have been signs / and I have tried to

KLYTEMNESTRA   And signs are scientific proof

AGAMEMNON   I know you're not behind me in my faith / we both know that, but

KLYTEMNESTRA   That's simplistic, that's a simplistic / version of what I think

AGAMEMNON   – but everything is pointing the same way

KLYTEMNESTRA   To kill our child. You're ill. You're mad. To kill our child?

AGAMEMNON   I wouldn't consider her / death – this is *why* I didn't say anything – I have looked for a way out, I *have* looked and looked and looked and looked –

KLYTEMNESTRA	'Her'! I am behind you, I have always been behind you, but Agamemnon, I don't *understand* how you could even think –
	All right. Stop. Tell me what you think is happening.
AGAMEMNON	I take her life by my own hand and then – we win the war.
	,
KLYTEMNESTRA	So why has she not fallen ill? Why can't the god just take her life himself?
AGAMEMNON	I don't *know* – but the signs are clear. I've asked again and again and the signs *are clear*.
KLYTEMNESTRA	I'm going to tell the truth. The signs aren't *real* – Agamemnon, it has to be the whole truth now before you [go ahead] – yes, you have a difficult life, a difficult job, and your father did – bad things *happened* to you, but life is hard, it is always hard, it is hard for everyone and your faith helps – I understand – I really do, but it's in your *head,* there isn't any evidence
AGAMEMNON	The whole world is evidence
KLYTEMNESTRA	The world in which you have to kill your child? But let's call god by his real name, tell the truth, call him the way we *actually* live our lives, the things you actually serve – call him money, call him power, call him wars against the weak –
AGAMEMNON	I'm trying to be honest and you *know* this war is a necessary evil, we are fighting an enemy that can't be / left unfought
KLYTEMNESTRA	Yes but the end result is people die. You kill people and people die. Put whatever words on it you like but it's killing people in order to take their things or prove them wrong or

'cause you don't like the people they are –
but let's be clear, those people die.

Look, it's good that we're here, it's good, it's
clearly what was meant to happen. There'll
be another way, another route, and we will
find it. This isn't right. Look at me. It's me.
Tell me this feels right.

,

AGAMEMNON   When did we, when did we when did we
decide that the right thing always *feels* right,
it doesn't, it's hard, it's it's destructive and
it's a sacrifice it's – putting yourself last, far
faraway last, cold at the back, in the service
of *other lives*, in the service of the greater
good

KLYTEMNESTRA The death of our child is not the greater good

AGAMEMNON   Their people, our people, the soldiers, you'd
have *them* die and all so she can live. But
we lose this war, and *my* daughter, she'll be
lucky if all she is is dead. And – what if she
dies and the wind comes?

KLYTEMNESTRA You don't *know that will happen*

AGAMEMNON   I know that someone has to win this war. I
didn't ask for this. You think I want to thrash
inside this net? I tried to think. I sought
advice. And now there's no more time. So
what do I do? What do you want me to do?

,

KLYTEMNESTRA I'm going to be sick. Your eyes are open –
and you choose your war. Your men. The
expression of the anger and the safety in
numbers, throwing ornate chairs through
thick glass windows, the women all begging
for mercy, and all signed off by the people
above you, you're men / you've *overcome*

AGAMEMNON	well, that is all just myth and actually there is no one above me
KLYTEMNESTRA	And this is about you, the leader, inhumanly committed –
AGAMEMNON	It isn't. It isn't that / at all.
KLYTEMNESTRA	Mr Noble. Mr Resolute. The hero, the *man* that does the *thing*
AGAMEMNON	It won't be made public – it's / not about us
KLYTEMNESTRA	Some part of you must recognize that, if it has to be a secret, then it's probably [a crime]
AGAMEMNON	I know how it sounds – but you cannot think one child – that *any* one child – is worth the loss of this war and this country and troops and / troops and troops
KLYTEMNESTRA	This is *my child.* She was a part of my body. I don't *feel* the people whose lives will be saved, this is our bright-eyed little daughter who wants to sing you her song or tell you her story or just – chatter. Remember when she was born? Remember that? I am not crying and – remember when they came to us and they said they weren't *sure* if she would *make it* and I – and just ignore this I'm I'm I'm / not crying
AGAMEMNON	This isn't about us
KLYTEMNESTRA	This is about you and me, this is about the state of our – I don't even know the word because it's not marriage, it's not union, not united – because the last thing we are, the last thing we are now is on the same side / but this *is* about us, this is about a person who came *from us,* who would never have *lived* if we hadn't loved each other, what you are / destroying is us, doing something that will overwhelm our history, a single

53

	action which if you bring it down on us will obliterate the whole story which precedes it
AGAMEMNON	Klytemnestra I need you to listen –
AGAMEMNON	Klytemnestra
KLYTEMNESTRA	She was a part of my body
AGAMEMNON	I don't want to do it
KLYTEMNESTRA	Then don't do it
	As her mother, I am begging you. I am begging you: find another way. There will [be] – there is another way. I know that you won't do this to your home.
AGAMEMNON	You're not the only mother

AGAMEMNON sneezes.

I asked for wisdom. And it came. It came from you. The child is the price of the war, and we don't see the price of the war, we don't see it, and this this will insist that I do, that my judgement is clear, the whole truth of it, that – we are a hurricane like the force of gods' own fury, ripping buildings into dust. We kill *their* children, their mothers are begging for mercy and – he said, 'you suffer, you learn'. And the child is the price of the war. It's knowing fully what our action *means*. The sacrifice of life begins at home.

,

KLYTEMNESTRA Sacrifice? This is slaughter, this is butchery – at this point, call it what you want but – smash a *bowl,* the bowl is smashed; she dies, your daughter dies, *Iphigenia* dies

I'm waking her up. I'll tell the house – I'll WAKE THE HOUSE and / get her out of bed and run

CILISSA is visible, awake, hearing this.

AGAMEMNON	Stop it, Klytemnestra, *stop,* you haven't got a chance
KLYTEMNESTRA	You're *killing* her. She won't *be here.* You're taking what's hers and it looks like *this,* this is destruction if you really want 'your judgement to be clear', we can just take what she loves and see what we learn from ripping it to pieces with our hands

KLYTEMNESTRA destroys IPHIGENIA's doll. He tries to stop her, get the toy back, she wrestles free. She physically pushes him.

AGAMEMNON	Stop it Klytemnestra / stop it, this isn't fair – give it *back*
KLYTEMNESTRA	Man resents child. He looks elsewhere. And you have made a fool of me for years. Of our marriage. For years. Don't think for a second that I didn't / know
AGAMEMNON	And what is that supposed to mean? [You stupid woman] has it been *a struggle* to live your life from the fruits of my success?
KLYTEMNESTRA	Are you going to *hit* me now? Do it – do it DO IT

KLYTEMNESTRA pushes his chest again – and he tries to restrain her and they fight – and it's ugly and it takes some time and she beats his back and eventually they fall apart from each other, breathing heavily. Both surprised by what has happened, by the speed at which their marriage has fractured.

,

Violence is how you've put food on our table. And that, I have allowed. What are you and I going to say to each other? How will you hug your son? How are you going to look at us once you come back home –

We hear crying. In this calm, KLYTEMNESTRA and AGAMEMNON have never felt so far apart.

It's / Orestes

AGAMEMNON	Orestes, I know.
	I'm sorry.
	,
	I wouldn't hurt you
KLYTEMNESTRA	In this conversation. That's an absurd thing to say.
	,
	God, it's so *hot* in here.

ORESTES is visible. He might have been listening.

ORESTES (Y)	I had a bad dream. Snakes.
	What's happening?
AGAMEMNON	Come here. Nothing's happening. You're not in trouble. It's over now.
KLYTEMNESTRA	It's over now? Orestes, honey, let me tell you what your daddy thinks, he thinks your bad dreams / are just the beginning, that they don't go away when you wake up, they swell inside
AGAMEMNON	*Don't.* They don't need to be involved –

ORESTES is caught between his parents.

KLYTEMNESTRA	You were always going to do it. You liked to push back against it – it's a good feeling, surrender, actually – but you knew, you knew from the first moment you heard – even before you heard the question – you knew what your answer would be. This was always going to happen.
	She's been dead since the beginning.

KLYTEMNESTRA's gone.

IPHIGENIA walks forward, looks at AGAMEMNON. A camera is set up, and AGAMEMNON notices.

AGAMEMNON	Is that / necessary?

MENELAUS   Yes. Yes. It's procedure, it's controlled,
                I'm – don't worry.

ORESTES and the DOCTOR.

ORESTES   I don't remember it. I was too young.

DOCTOR   That's all right. What are you holding?

ORESTES   A silver tray on which are three small,
                pleated paper cups.

EXHIBIT: SILVER TRAY WITH THREE PAPER CUPS

AGAMEMNON *has* IPHIGENIA *on his knee.* MENELAUS *and another
woman also present. The camera is switched on.*

WOMAN   Iphigenia. What a beautiful name.

MENELAUS   Are we ready?

                ,

WOMAN   I need you to confirm as Iphigenia's guardian
                that you fully understand the course of action
                in front of her today, and that you consent.
                I need you to / clearly conf

AGAMEMNON   Yes. Yes. Yes. Yes.

MENELAUS   She has to – ask the questions. It has to be
                done.

WOMAN   I need you to clearly confirm that you
                understand the procedure.

AGAMEMNON   I understand.

WOMAN   And I need you to confirm that you know
                what will happen as a result of the procedure.

AGAMEMNON   I know.

WOMAN   Thank you. OK.

                ,

                Right, Iphigenia. You're doing very well.
                I need you to drink this.

IPHIGENIA sits on AGAMEMNON's knee. Looks at him for confirmation. He nods. If he could say something, he probably would. He can't.

ORESTES   One of them contains a small amount of translucent liquid.

AGAMEMNON gives her, and IPHIGENIA drinks, the contents of the first cup.

WOMAN   And now just swallow this one. Try and make it just one swallow, straight down. It's not a nice taste, so you might need this one afterwards.

ORESTES   The second one contains a small orange tablet. The third one a sweet-flavoured liquid. Inside that tablet somewhere, one atom – makes it too much, tips the balance.

AGAMEMNON takes the tablet from the second cup and puts it on IPHIGENIA's tongue. She swallows it. It's bitter, and she crumples the cup. She's given the third one.

WOMAN   Very good. Well done. You're a very brave girl.

,

There's a long, long, long, long sharp pause. Total stillness and silence. We're waiting for the child to die.

AGAMEMNON   I love / you

IPHIGENIA   I think now I want to lie down.

She stretches out across AGAMEMNON. Eyes closed. Another long pause.

He suddenly lifts her up and he holds her tight, protective, impossible to believe he's here. As he resettles with her, she's drowsy, incoherent, but looks right at him and says something that's clearly discernable as

water, Daddy ... water.

AGAMEMNON makes to get it for her –

MENELAUS   No, we can't, that's not –

             – and AGAMEMNON would get it, except her eyes have already closed. There's another long pause. Then:

             IPHIGENIA. TIME OF DEATH: [[TODAY'S DATE, THE TIME]].

WOMAN   She's gone.

             Do you feel / alright?

AGAMEMNON   I feel like I've done something so wrong that my whole life, my family, nothing will be able to – the worst mistake. The worst mistake. I got it wrong. It was wrong. It was wrong.

             But the last bit of this is drowned out the sound of the wind, real wind. Doors and windows rattle and fly open and the still, heavy heat is ruptured by cold wind flooding like a tide through the theatre.

             KLYTEMNESTRA steps forward in front of this, she's heard the wind, realizing something. In a moment, she will scream.

             IPHIGENIA's body is carried away.

             The wind rages now. Paper, fabric, lamps go flying, anything not fixed down, blows all over the set. KLYTEMNESTRA stands in full blast of it.

             CALCHAS reads the facts.

CALCHAS   Areas of very high pressure circling down onto us, and the winds are picking up across the whole of the West now, so there's quite a time ahead for us, I'm afraid, it looks like this sudden onset is likely to remain with us, and even in the weeks to come, these systems seem reluctant to fade away so we'll be living with them for some time. Good night.

             Wind rumbles underneath, distant, restless.

DOCTOR   Orestes. Do you remember the words you used – before?

ORESTES   Beating in the sky. The wind.

DOCTOR   The mother hare, it's Klytemnestra, the
                    eagles are the men and the dead child inside
                    the womb – It was *this story*. Her story.
                    Iphigenia.

The stage is a mess. AGAMEMNON enters, sees KLYTEMNESTRA.

AGAMEMNON   Did you [make all this mess] – ?

KLYTEMNESTRA   Yes. Don't worry, you're safe, it's over now.

AGAMEMNON   There is a statement. Natural causes, deep /
                    shock, asking for privacy –

KLYTEMNESTRA   I heard. And the wind.

                    ,

He makes to leave, when:

                    I'm really quite tired, but I want you to know
                    that I – I won't say this tomorrow or again,
                    perhaps. But

*Perhaps KLYTEMNESTRA stands behind him, puts her arms
around his waist.*

                    I admire it. Somewhere. The decision.

                    It's so autistically brave.

AGAMEMNON   Don't – [make a fuss]

KLYTEMNESTRA   I'm not, I won't. I mean: I mean it.

AGAMEMNON   It's hard not to interpret that as –

KLYTEMNESTRA   Let's just hold off the interpretation tonight.

                    I know you feel it. I know it was hard. I do
                    know that.

                    And I do love you

                    ,

                    You're not going to come back, are you?

                    If it doesn't claim you – once you've won this
                    war, once we've played the happy couple,

you're going to leave. It's all right. I would prefer the truth.

You're not intending to come home, not to us. Not now.

AGAMEMNON   I don't know, there's no need to be [rash], it could be years before –

KLYTEMNESTRA   But –

AGAMEMNON   No.

KLYTEMNESTRA   Thank you.

,

AGAMEMNON   I don't want that to imply any criticism / of you or the way

KLYTEMNESTRA   Don't. Don't.

Go to sleep. I won't come up tonight. Please. Tomorrow this will all be fresh history. You will be setting out across the water. And I will get up at the very first sign of morning, and I will make a plan.

He kisses her gently, no reaction, he leaves. She sits for a while entirely alone on the stage. Maybe quite a while.

CALCHAS   Please be upstanding. We pause there for the first time. Thank you.

The act is over.

ACT TWO

ORESTES I watch it again, happening for the first time but – too late, too late to stop it. It pours out of me. But what if what's next is – ? What if it's better left sealed up, undisturbed?

DOCTOR It's what you feel. We have to understand the truth.

ORESTES What if it's a dream? What if it's a lie?

DOCTOR Then those lies reveal something about you. 'Our self' isn't an absolute thing. It's handfuls of memories and moments and people – and we form them into who we think we are. For most of us, it's only partly true: one version of truth. / A story.

ORESTES A story. A story I've been through before. As a child. But I don't know where it ends –

DOCTOR To be a child is not to know what went before you. And we know where this started, Orestes, we stopped at what happened to your sister.

ORESTES She died. Iphigenia.

KLYTEMNESTRA still in position as at the end of the first act.
IPHIGENIA stands where KLYTEMNESTRA can see her. She's dead, but she looks exactly as she did in the first act.

KLYTEMNESTRA This whole thing, this whole thing is about you.

IPHIGENIA is gone.

DOCTOR You look tired.

ORESTES Thank you. I try to sleep. I have bad dreams. Why is that? Which cell is that carved into? Some people just sleep.

CALCHAS reads the facts.

CALCHAS   … foreign stations are suggesting, though
                 at this stage there is no official news or any
                 formal statement. Good morning. Details
                 are still coming in, but early reports are
                 suggesting significant news concerning our
                 troops and what may mark a significant
                 watershed in this conflict …

There are sudden loud fireworks.

ORESTES   The war takes years. Much longer than
                 they'd thought. And – we don't know what
                 to believe –

ELECTRA   So how do you decide?

ORESTES   Electra. Electra would know what to do.

More fireworks.

ELECTRA   Wake up. Wake *up.* It's true.

ORESTES   What's happening?

ELECTRA   Wake up. It's happened. Last night.
                 It happened. I don't know whether to believe
                 it or not but it's what everyone's saying.

ORESTES   Don't kiss / me.

ELECTRA   I can kiss you if it's good news

ORESTES   What's happened?

ELECTRA   We won.

ORESTES   We – what? How do you know?

ELECTRA   Mum said. The war, we've won. It means
                 Dad's coming home.

*Suddenly the atmosphere of preparation, distant bands play,
smoke in the air, we're outside, people rushing everywhere
preparing for a major public event. ORESTES sees his mother,
being prepared for interview.*

ORESTES   Mum … say hello … say hello … wave …

KLYTEMNESTRA	I want you to remember today. This is one of the good days. This is an important day.
ORESTES	When did we win? How did you know?
KLYTEMNESTRA	I know. We won. They're all on their way home. And your father.
ORESTES	Are you pleased?
KLYTEMNESTRA	I'm delighted, Orestes. I'm ecstatic. Are you pleased?
ORESTES	Yes.
	But how do you know that we won? I don't want to believe it until I *know* it's true, because if it / isn't, then I –
KLYTEMNESTRA	I'm sure. You don't need to / doubt
ORESTES	But is there evidence? Was there any sign? Did you dream it?
	,
KLYTEMNESTRA	Dream? I'm not a child. Are you going to question your father like this? And there are always signs. You just have to know how to read them.
ORESTES	How?
KLYTEMNESTRA	Why do we call that thing a 'chair'? It's just sounds in the air, strange black symbols on white paper. Chair. But you and I both know the code – that word – 'chair' – points to that thing. *This* means *that*.
	I have come to realise that everything, my darling, is about the connections between things, between – word and deed, inside and outside. One person and another.
	Once it was signal fires. Lit in one place, the light seen miles away. Then that became

'if it's a yes, go to the window and light the
lamp' – like in the story, you remember?

ORESTES   Yes

KLYTEMNESTRA   And it's still light. Light inside your brain,
impulses, burning, firing forwards, carrying
signs – continuous light – but smaller
even than we can see it, fired up inside the
hollow of the walls, sweeping under the
floors and up over the roofs and bouncing
distantly unbroken in the sky, and so *fast,*
so inconceivably impossibly fast, splitting
a second into a thousand parts. And,
this moment, now, there are so many
infinitesimal points on the globe ablaze, so
many rapid lines of light, connecting 1 to 2
to 3, lines shimmering and intertwining and
reweaving themselves, that we have wrought
a net which holds the world, illuminating like
another sun.

And the moment that war ends, the final
occupation is complete, on the ground,
there – one signal is sent, then another
signal screaming through the lines of this
massive invisible structure, like runners in
a relay race, cutting across the deep buzz of
civilisation – to this house and this room and
this hand – and with a little click –

The sign. And you read. And you judge. And
you know. Just like that 'chair'.

I know where the bases were, what roads
they took, what weapons they used, that
it was too hot for the most part to wear a
uniform. And I know for a fact that we've
won.

DOCTOR   Why have you stopped?

ORESTES   There's a way of reading the signs –
           gathering little things up into big slabs of
           meaning – but it just slips. There's things
           missing.

DOCTOR   Are you talking about your sister?

ORESTES   No. I don't – no. It's what came next –

*KLYTEMNESTRA is interviewed. She is more open in public
than in private.*

QUESTION   I will understand if there are things you don't
           want to say.

KLYTEMNESTRA   I'm happy to talk about my family, I'm not
           ashamed at all. I love my husband. I love my
           husband. And I can't tell you what it means
           to welcome him home. I've been the man of
           the house, keeping the home fires burning.
           And now. HE'S COMING HOME. God,
           I'm not ashamed to shout that from the
           rooftops – it's the, time really doesn't do
           wonders for modesty.

QUESTION   But it hasn't been an easy time for you?

KLYTEMNESTRA   How could it ever be easy?

QUESTION   Your husband left only days after the tragic
           passing of your daughter, of Iphi*gen*ia.

KLYTEMNESTRA   Iphigen*i*-a. Yes.

QUESTION   That must have been hard.

KLYTEMNESTRA   Just – look at my face. I'm an old woman
           now. You cry. You pull yourself together. You
           see her clothes in the wardrobe. You see *his*
           clothes. You cry. You try to sleep, but, the
           tiniest sound, a fly beats its wings and your
           eyes crack back open.

           Which is to say, you live alone in the house,
           yes, but where you're really alone is inside
           your head. You dream the worst. It's not

helped by the age we live in – there are
the rumours, of course, and if he had been
wounded every time it was reported, there'd
be more holes than flesh, like a net (!) or
something – you can't trust what's being said
– [but] you can't ignore it either. It worms
its way in. Relentlessly imagining his death.
You walk the halls, you wait for it to come.
An arrival, the bell rings – some stranger,
formal – and you know what he's here for as
soon as the door swings open. But the stories,
the endless cacophony of judgement – even
today when the news first came, people
said 'don't rejoice too early, typical woman,
jumping to conclusions' – it doesn't help
anything.

QUESTION   Of course. And that has affected your health.

KLYTEMNESTRA   Yes, it has.

,

QUESTION   Which is something you've been very brave
in discussing.

KLYTEMNESTRA   Thank you. I thought it was important –
important to speak about the pressure at
home. You're being very, well, dignified in
not saying it, but, for those who haven't read
between the lines, I attempted suicide. I tried
to hang myself.

,

QUESTION   Yes. But you're doing better now. Your
mental / health

KLYTEMNESTRA   I'm not sure that's – well, I'm not sure it's
really a *medical* thing, I mean it's not an
irrational response, given the position in
which I found myself. Who knows?

67

But yes. I am in full command now. You protect your children.

QUESTION   Your husband has been fighting for several years now, and under his command our forces have, as you know, suffered substantial losses. I wondered whether you thought he might feel in some way / responsible

KLYTEMNESTRA   I wouldn't know about that. I'm his wife, not his conscience.

QUESTION   You wouldn't know?

KLYTEMNESTRA   I've been in this house. I haven't seen him.

,

QUESTION   But as a woman, you must have an opinion? These are people's / children

KLYTEMNESTRA   'As a woman'. I find that a disquieting phrase. I mean, I don't have sets of opinions depending on the mask I'm wearing, it's not as if I think one thing when I'm – breastfeeding and then change entirely when I'm doing something – I mean, I can't answer you *as a woman*. I contain multitudes. I'm not sure how much being a woman means to me. I've never been a man. My gender isn't something I selected for myself; it doesn't surprise me when I look in the mirror.

QUESTION   Yes – I'm sure you are aware of the reports: alleged incidents abroad, the violations of civilian homes and places of worship in the / final stages

KLYTEMNESTRA   I've heard reports, like everyone else. What none of us know yet is the truth – and so what we say is merely speculation. I'll wait for clearer information before I assume to judge.

QUESTION	Finally, what does today mean?
KLYTEMNESTRA	Who wrote your questions? Well, it means something different to each of us. The war is finished, that's the – fact – if you like, but we all look at that fact through our own lens, our own families, our own dreams and sadnesses. To me? What does it mean? Too much. Let's just say that it's an extraordinary *relief* that today is here, finally here.
QUESTION	Thank you. I know you'll need to prepare – we're expecting them to reach us at any moment –
KLYTEMNESTRA	Thank *you*.
ORESTES	You watch yourself like in a dream, it's like watching someone else, you're walking back along the road, but the trap is still a shock the second time, you have to fall into the trap – the trap is yours. That's stupid, isn't it?
DOCTOR	No. I'm here to help you. I'm not here to judge you.
ORESTES	It was solid, then. And now it crumbles – it breaks into memory – and I force the pieces back but they're all in different places and it doesn't work, there's holes. The thing won't *hold.* There's something *wrong.*
DOCTOR	Just tell me what happens. One step at a time.
ORESTES	He comes home.

AGAMEMNON enters. He looks older, greyer. He's been through a lot.

KLYTEMNESTRA looks at him. She moves swiftly to him, hugs him. It takes some time for her to let go. They move to a podium and address the crowds.

KLYTEMNESTRA	Before we begin our lives again, before we take the time for this family to heal, I just

have a few things to say. God, you're so used
to hearing these speeches, so well-trodden,
but it's different when you're here.

This is a happy day, but it cannot be a day
entirely without sadness. As we celebrate, we
think of those who will not be at home today,
and we think of those families who are not
welcoming home their hero, and we think
of the empty chair at their table tonight. To
them, I say this: we are all, every one of
us, all your families. Around the world. We
stretch our hands out to hold yours. We share
your loss. We mourn your loss. We honour
their sacrifice.

And as for those who come back to us today,
we are truly lucky, but their trials are not
yet over. They have made it to the opposite
bank, but now they have to turn around,
swim back home, to climb back out where
they first dived in. As these soldiers once
more become accustomed to the way they
used to live, keep them well. Allow them
to fall backward into the embrace of their
homes.

And this house too has missed the head
of its table. Whatever he is to you, inside,
he's just another husband, another father.
Another man. The best of men. My hero. My
husband.

AGAMEMNON Well. Your speech, like my, uh, absence,
went on for longer than perhaps –

(He laughs.) – I'm happy to be home, though
I think, my wife is perhaps not best placed to
praise me, for –

'

I'm not going to cry or anything.

We won. We got them. It happened.

And we are all thankful to be home. It's in
the lap of the gods – and we've been *lucky*,
to win, to return, to – look, it came down on
our side and we are *thankful* for that. The city
god didn't favour – well, she's not a city any
more.

It's a hard place to be. The heat, especially
and the sand, the lice. You miss a cold tap
that's actually cold. Even in the winter
it's not cold but the birds die, somehow –
couldn't figure out why that happened but
they're everywhere, strange feathered lumps
all over the roads. But we have remained
unified: it's a hard thing to do to look on
other people's success and be happy for
them, no jealousy, no bitterness – and that's
the sort of company I am lucky to have had.
That's the truth. There are some of us who
haven't come back, as she [said] – including
my brother, who sadly, uh, as I'm sure you
know. So.

MENELAUS. TIME OF DEATH: [[TODAY'S DATE, THE TIME]].

There's a lot of work to do to put our house
in order. There are many things that will
need our intervention – we'll be asking
where things have gone wrong, and taking
whatever action necessary to put things right.
Which will include the healing of the sick.

I was also, uh, moved, by some of the
civilians, the ordinary people over there,
after – one of whom I've brought home,
at my own expense. She's only a girl, her
family were sadly, uh, [casualties], and
she's – she was hidden in a church when we
found her, knees bleeding on the stonefloor,
underneath the altar, shaking – and I wanted

71

to save her, Cassandra, she's [called] – she's not yet ready to speak in public but she will, in time, and I think her story will be important for all of us to hear. Because I understand – it's important to remember – that victory was dearly bought – is, always.

All right. Thank you. To all of you. For your support and prayers. To my family. And bringing us safely home was gods' work and for that I say – thank you.

KLYTEMNESTRA Thank you for coming back. In so many ways, it's been a long journey – and now there are only a few steps left. We all wanted those steps to be soft – for you to walk in on a river of scarlet – we wanted to do justice to you – to give you a just welcome home.

A carpet is spread out for AGAMEMNON to walk in on.

AGAMEMNON It's not right

KLYTEMNESTRA It's your right – and no one would deny it

AGAMEMNON It's a red carpet – I'm not a priest – it's wrong

KLYTEMNESTRA It's a welcome home – and those times over there when you longed to be here, it's something that you'd have *sworn* to do. It's what the enemy would be doing / if he was in your shoes

AGAMEMNON It's extravagance – expensive cloth – I don't like how it looks

KLYTEMNESTRA It's not for you to be led by jealousy

AGAMEMNON This shouldn't be a fight

KLYTEMNESTRA Then surrender: you don't need to win

AGAMEMNON Does it really mean that much?

AGAMEMNON smiles, tired.

Let the record show that she made me do it.
I'll take my shoes off. I'm not sure I can walk
on this. It's about as extravagant as I am
ashamed. I – I don't like taking curtain calls.

KLYTEMNESTRA   I'm sorry. Don't prepare to come inside. You
don't get to come inside the house.

AGAMEMNON   Thank you.

AGAMEMNON takes a single step onto the red carpet.

,

ORESTES   My breath smells of fear. I feel like there's
a bird inside me beating to get out. I *know* I
know what's coming – but I don't.

DOCTOR   What are you scared of?

ORESTES   What *happens* when I dream? What is
knotting together with what – what is being
made? Fear and wishes and – and if it's
me, if it's just inside me with no meaning
elsewhere, can't I create something *better*
than this, can't I choose imagined hope
rather than imagined fear?

DOCTOR   Perhaps the fear is real.

ORESTES   Is it? Is it illusion? How do I know?

I feel like everything is *full*, interwoven,
significant – and it goes so fast, a white sea
of eyes and every single person there, every
single person now alive will be dead in –
what in historical terms is no time at all. And
what does it *mean*?

DOCTOR   Just – tell me what happens

ORESTES   I look up and it's like my heart is pumping
out the blue of the clouds hot onto my face

*AGAMEMNON first one inside, same position as before, same
words:*

AGAMEMNON   I'm home.

He touches the table. Looks back around the house. It's familiar, though years and years have passed. And then KLYTEMNESTRA *is inside. It's difficult to tell what their relationship is now.*

What was that supposed to mean?

,

KLYTEMNESTRA *goes up to him, almost aggressive. She takes his head, rests it against her forehead. Then she kisses him, hungrily. He kisses her back. Maybe they'll have sex. But then they don't. And he says:*

There's so much to say, I –

CILISSA *is there. She has* AGAMEMNON'S *dressing gown. He puts it on.*

ORESTES	It's like a net of animals hoisted above you and it's going to split and they'll fall onto [you] – but it's too high for you to see what animals are in there now, you can just hear them and slightly smell them but you're not sure whether it's snakes or birds or fish or what – and you just – you think – I want one to slip through, to drop down into my hands – and then at least I'd know –
	Does that mean anything?
DOCTOR	Yes / of course.
ORESTES	Or a sea of fluid slapping against the weakest wall of a room, trickles running down the cracks, tiny shudders, any moment it smashes through –
DOCTOR	Are you scared of your father?
ORESTES	I can't get it. I can't get it.
DOCTOR	I need you tell me the truth. What happens?
KLYTEMNESTRA	And it's a simple task: it shouldn't take hours.
CILISSA	And what shall I do with his clothes?

KLYTEMNESTRA	Anything stained, just – actually, throw them all out.

CILISSA and ELECTRA try and bring in CASSANDRA. She wears a saffron dress, and is reminiscent somehow of IPHIGENIA.

CILISSA	It all comes home. She's a prisoner of war – she'll fit right in. Come on.
ELECTRA	You can come in. You can come into the house now.
CILISSA	Your mother doesn't want her seen.
ELECTRA	Hello? Speak? Come. In. DO. YOU. SPEAK?
CILISSA	Like a wild animal.
ELECTRA	She won't speak the same language as us.
CILISSA	Oh, I think she understands us. I think she's angry. Angry to be away from home, angry to be trapped.
	I feel sorry for her.
	Make a sign. If you understand. Make a sign.

ORESTES and DOCTOR.

DOCTOR	We have to accept that our parents are people. No greater or better than us. Just people, at the end.
ORESTES	But they *created* you. They made you, they're – they're more than human if they – they're creators. Your creators. Mythic.
DOCTOR	That's true for all of us.
ORESTES	Dinner. The family.

KLYTEMNESTRA rings the dinner bell. The family assemble. The table is set again: a version of the same ritual. CASSANDRA sits in IPHIGENIA's seat, takes her place. Deep unease with this stranger at the table. Everyone looking at her.

KLYTEMNESTRA	What's your name?

	You're the foreign import, are you?
ELECTRA	She doesn't speak.
KLYTEMNESTRA	I can't blame her for that.
AGAMEMNON	Be kind to her. She won't be here for long.

,

ELECTRA	Dad. What's going on?
KLYTEMNESTRA	That's an interesting question.
AGAMEMNON	I have had *enough* of being questioned, everyone.
ORESTES	Dinner in silence. Wine.

ELECTRA uncorks and pours wine.

ELECTRA	It's better at least than the old tell the story of your day thing, do you / remember
ORESTES	Electra.
	It's like the ghost of how we used to be, the family, years earlier, that ghost is fluid up to our [waists] and we're moving around in it … it's all new but the feeling is just behind our heads
DOCTOR	That's good. Old feelings. Strong feelings.
ORESTES	I want to stop.
DOCTOR	We can't stop. What happens?
ORESTES	It ends. Dinner ends.

As they rise from the table, AGAMEMNON speaks to KLYTEMNESTRA.

AGAMEMNON	I miss her. It's strange without her here. You can feel the … the – I don't have the word.
ORESTES	More must have happened, it's all rushing, I can't – it's rushing forward in my head. More was said. We're here too soon.
AGAMEMNON	We will talk later. About everything. I'm going to take a bath.

CILISSA has started the bath running. ELECTRA knocks on the table. CASSANDRA becomes gradually more frenzied.

ELECTRA   Why do you keep swallowing?

What happened to you?

Did you even want to come here?

,

Is my dad fucking you? Are you in love?

ORESTES   Can you ever know you're going to do something *before* it happens – there are too many little things that can throw it all off course, everything has an effect –

ELECTRA   *Can you actually speak?*

Then: CASSANDRA suddenly speaks in Ancient Greek from the original Aeschylus – passionate, furious, tearful. It's terrifying to listen to.

CASSANDRA   οτοτοτοο ϖόϖοι δο

ORESTES and ELECTRA jump.

ORESTES   She speaks, but I don't understand her, it's another / world

CASSANDRA now continues to speak in Ancient Greek underneath the below.

ELECTRA   *(Ad lib.)* I don't understand you – I don't know what you're saying.

ORESTES   It's too much – like the blood rushing to my heart. I'm pale, I can feel myself feeling dizzy – I don't remember specifically what – I don't have *access* –

Is this what I felt then or what I'm feeling now?

DOCTOR   I don't know what you think the difference is

ORESTES   Why do we do things?

DOCTOR   What do you mean?

ORESTES   Is it because we – can you predict based on
                       our parents and our actions and our – every
                       single day is another another – can you
                       know, can you ever know, what someone is
                       going to do until it's done?

AGAMEMNON has a thought. He's remembering IPHIGENIA.

AGAMEMNON   I'd like to hear some / music.

ORESTES   Music.

*We hear IPHIGENIA's song in its original recording. It plays
underneath the below action – an accumulation of sounds
now, fighting for dominance.*

*As AGAMEMNON reaches the bathroom, IPHIGENIA is sitting at
the end of the bath. The little girl in the yellow dress. Their
eyes meet. He shakes his head, eyes full of tears.*

CASSANDRA suddenly speaks in English:

CASSANDRA   catched in trap. same story. it's same story
                       doesn't stop doesn't cease it's same same
                       story my story is your story is – family
                       extinct – only survivor – father after father
                       the blood runs down, seeps thick through the
                       generations, hangs over house like a blanket,
                       house beats like heart hearth it all burns
                       turns blisters the blood the line the word
                       a net a web a trap and fury is already here
                       inside, screaming children / already inside

ELECTRA   You're mad. You're seeing things. There's
                       nothing / there

CASSANDRA   the house breathes slaughter. he dies.
                       murder. he dies now. no good gods here.
                       not in this story. these are his final moments.
                       these ones. he dies now.

ELECTRA   WHO dies? Who's died? I don't /
                       understand

CASSANDRA   can you hear the singing? they are all singing
                       in this house, always in the house, in every

room, smells of the grave, sweet, salty, thick,
the open ground. thick, warm blood sweeps
through the house, splashes up the walls, like
oil across the floor, there's no way out, no
way back

Elsewhere, KLYTEMNESTRA *addresses* CILISSA.

KLYTEMNESTRA   I wonder at what point you'll actually wake
up.

CASSANDRA   i try to tell you – i *know*. i know you. you're
in the same place as i am – taste the iron
in the air. and look. the child outstretches
handsfull of flesh.

please don't forget me. it is written, written
in clear black – everywhere dead girls. dead
girls.

CASSANDRA   / the sadness washes all the rest away

ORESTES   the sadness washes all the rest away: I
remember –

*The playback speed of the music gets sickeningly faster and
faster.*

DOCTOR   What are you holding?

ORESTES   It's a knife, a knife – that – it's silver, long-
bladed, it has a maker, 'lábrys', engraved on
the [handle] –

EXHIBIT: SILVER LÁBRYS KNIFE

AGAMEMNON *gets into the bath – the sense of something finally
completed.*

I – I know what happens.

KLYTEMNESTRA *whips the tablecloth off the table. Walks to
the bathroom.*

AGAMEMNON *sees her, conciliatory. She enters and calmly
throws the cloth over his head and stabs him. We don't see
it, but he falls hard against the bath. She stabs him again
and again and again.*

ORESTES The girl is dead. I don't – remember how she died

CASSANDRA lies to one side. Blood runs from the corner of her mouth.

CASSANDRA. TIME OF DEATH: [[TODAY'S DATE, THE TIME]].

I stand right there and my first thought is I should call Dad, I should ask God, I – where's Electra? – Electra would know what to do – and things congeal, the moments thicken – I don't know where to cast my vote – not sure enough to judge or know what to do – and though it's slower now, I do nothing – and it's already done. It's her. It's *her*.

It's suddenly silent. The music stops.

AGAMEMNON. TIME OF DEATH: [[TODAY'S DATE, THE TIME]].

Then, KLYTEMNESTRA comes very precisely out of the bathroom, dragging the body of AGAMEMNON into view covered in bathwater and blood. AGAMEMNON's body continues to bleed.

KLYTEMNESTRA There … there … there … there … there … there are some things to say now, some things to –

KLYTEMNESTRA is entirely rational, quiet, collected, forceful.

Everything I have said until this point – all of it – was lies. To myself, to my family, to the public, to *him,* it was all, all untrue but as I speak this, in this moment, this *is* true – from now.

'Killed by his *wife*.' Not a person. Not a murderer. A woman. Because we love a female criminal, that *strength* a transgression, carnal, sexier or some[thing], the stronger-weaker vessel or [whatever] – but this is not the world. Not now. The lights are on. Your houses have drawers full of knives. It's not biology, not destiny, it's just – *balance,* the law of *moral appetite,* the inevitable act that follows when when when – he killed our daughter. He killed our daughter, my daughter that I carried in my body. And so this right hand had the right to strike – and it struck. It struck his foreign bitch and it struck him down.

The war came home. This is what he *did:* this is the war that put food on our table. This is how it *looks.* What did you think was inside that word? You know this is what happens, what it looks like, this is the human animal panicking as the cord is cut – and you can look away but he did this thing, in your name, to our enemies, and he did it to our daughter, did this to her, set the thing in motion, and now *just* is the *balance* of his act.

– and when the life, struggling out of him, sprayed by lumps of blood, blood hitting blood on my neck and down my arms and soaking up my clothes but god it was *something* it did not disgust me not even for a second – the rhythm of it – the way it slid into him – god it was so fucking *easy* – even just thinking it I want to do it again, I want another *ride,* I want it always – *now* – I want the *(Scream.)* of it all – and I open my mouth like a plant in the rain in the red and I feel so awake, it's like liquid *rightness* pumping into arteries, he's *dead,* I am alive – and I'm free – and from this point, from now, this house is set in order ONCE AND FOR ALL

CALCHAS Please be upstanding. We will now take a pause. Thank you.

The act is over. The body is removed.

ACT THREE

The sound of wind. The feel: grey morning. CILISSA *is cleaning.*

KLYTEMNESTRA lifts the dinner bell, doesn't ring it.

ELECTRA We don't have to do that any more. We could just break the habit. We could just stop.

KLYTEMNESTRA It's a tradition, not a habit.

ELECTRA What's the difference?

KLYTEMNESTRA Whether or not it means anything.

KLYTEMNESTRA rings the dinner bell. KLYTEMNESTRA and ELECTRA sit down. The tablecloth has holes in it and the bloodstains are now dried.

DOCTOR Orestes, we need to keep going. We need to establish what happened. The whole truth of / what happened

ORESTES He died. She killed him.

DOCTOR And you survived that trauma. Life went on afterwards – and now it's something that *happened* – and that isn't easy. We're barely *there* in the moment it blossoms – we hardly *feel* it as it hollows us out – what hurts is the *next* second; awakening into what's *left* –

And I don't think you've woken up. I'm not sure you want to wake up.

ORESTES Why would / I

DOCTOR Fear. Of where you might be. Where you might really be.

IPHIGENIA stands on the table, dancing.

KLYTEMNESTRA There are a certain few people in a life that you *absorb*, they stay alive in you, even after they've [gone], ideas, what they would *think*, their way of laughing –– and by my age you

82

have them in place. And your connection
with them is so strong, that splitting, when it
comes, will be violent. It can't not be violent.
They made you.

And losing them, you lose a part of yourself.
We are so horribly tied to each other,
so bound up together. And as you [lose
someone], as they fall over the edge some
invisible cord pulls tight, and rips a huge
lump out from under your skin.

I miss him. I know you think I don't feel
anything, that I'm … but the person who
knew you when you were young and
beautiful, loved you when you were. Well,
you only get one of those.

My brain still thinks she's here. Even now. I
thought it would stop. This house so silent. I
keep thinking I can smell her hair –

Are you wearing her dress?

Are you?

ELECTRA	Why shouldn't I?
KLYTEMNESTRA	Because it's wrong. It isn't – civilised. Take her clothes off. Take them *off*. It isn't right.
ELECTRA	They're there. There's no one to wear them now.
KLYTEMNESTRA	They're not *for you*. It's sick.
ELECTRA	Fine. But it's the moment the dress goes over your head. Wrapped in cloth. You're blind. Vulnerable.
KLYTEMNESTRA	Just words, [honey]. Just words.
ELECTRA	Iphigenia. Natural causes. Agamemnon. Natural causes.

*Enter AEGISTHUS, late. He takes his place at the table. He is
played by the same actor who played AGAMEMNON.*

AEGISTHUS   Sorry, sorry for lateness.

ELECTRA   If you're not here, you don't eat

ELECTRA opens wine, easily now.

CILISSA is staring sort of intensely at AEGISTHUS.

KLYTEMNESTRA   She doesn't remember *anything.* Your brain is
                 holed below the water line –

She gives up. What's the point.

                 (Slow, loud.) This is Aegisthus. You've seen
                 him before. And now you can go and look
                 for dust again.

CILISSA   The man of the house. My lady, I am having
                 a bit of trouble with the house, the stains
                 won't / wash away

KLYTEMNESTRA   I am sick of you telling me this. Really, really
                 sick.

CILISSA leaves.

                 I don't like the way she looks at people. I've
                 never liked it.

ELECTRA   At what point is the house going to be
                 unlocked? And why are we not talking about
                 Orestes? Why are you not worried? He's
                 gone. He's been gone for –

                 ,

AEGISTHUS   It's nice to eat all together like this.

                 And it's a delicious meal.

DOCTOR   So when did Aegisthus arrive?

ORESTES   I don't know.

DOCTOR   Was it before your father's passing? Did
                 Aegisthus play a part in your father's /
                 death?

ORESTES   I don't *know.*

DOCTOR   And he was your mother's lover? He was in the house?

ORESTES   Yes.

Though only a few moments earlier the actor was playing AEGISTHUS, he now becomes AGAMEMNON and ELECTRA talks to him.

ELECTRA   Dad. You used to sit right there.

AGAMEMNON   I did. Family meals. Your mother's custom. Still going.

ELECTRA   We're not the model family of the modern major general. But then we weren't that when you were here either.

It's strange that you aren't here.

AGAMEMNON   You'll get used to it.

ELECTRA   I haven't yet.

AGAMEMNON   You will.

ELECTRA   It feels like minutes. I know it's been longer than that.

AGAMEMNON   This is it now. This is doing things fatherless.

ELECTRA   I just thought that.

AGAMEMNON   Like father [like son].

ELECTRA   I sharpen my pencil fatherless. I pour a glass of wine fatherless. I don't drink it fatherless. I hear a song fatherless that I used to [like] –

I feel absolutely nothing at all.

I imagine a conversation with my father fatherless. The colour of it stains my head. It echoes. It stays with me. Whether or not any of the words were ever spoken, it's the realest thing that happens all day.

AGAMEMNON   It isn't easy. But it will be worth it.

ELECTRA   Ah, you're not really there.

AGAMEMNON	Neither are you, most of the time.
ELECTRA	Now what does *that* mean?

AGAMEMNON smiles.

	I feel betrayed by the house. I want it to be crushed into wreckage, but it just stays the same. Locked.
AGAMEMNON	I know it's hard. It's really hard. But in some ways it's better like this than it was before. We're better like this.
ELECTRA	At least we talk now. Before you were like a god or something. As in, I asked for things and you ignored me.
	What do you miss the most being dead?
AGAMEMNON	Red wine, probably.
ELECTRA	I miss *you*.
	,
AGAMEMNON	You don't need me. It's all ahead of you. Old age. Before that, children. Before that, marriage. Before that, falling in love for the first time.
ELECTRA	I think that happened. Did you fall in love with mum?
AGAMEMNON	Yes.
ELECTRA	And the others?
AGAMEMNON	Yes.
ELECTRA	I don't understand.
AGAMEMNON	Why does it have to be only one thing? Can it not be more?
	,
ELECTRA	Did you believe in god – the storey above – did you believe all that because you were scared? Or because you really believed?

AGAMEMNON	What's the difference?
ELECTRA	You see, I think there is one.
	I don't drink any more. I did for a while. But the pain sort of soaks through the wine and it doesn't really taste like anything.
AGAMEMNON	You got used to wine.
ELECTRA	I did.
	I wonder a lot about what it's all for. What it all means.

AGAMEMNON slowly gets up, leaves.

	And this doesn't really work because you're not really there. And the second I'm conscious of that, properly conscious, you're not there at all. You're just a guest in my imagination – some diluted performance of you replaying and replaying and replaying
ORESTES	I want to *stop*.
DOCTOR	That isn't possible: we have to try and understand the truth
ORESTES	This is *my life* – and I do not want to talk about the truth, there isn't one, there are just versions of versions, twisting variations, seething over each other like bees, and one of them actually happened, there's one that is actually *right*
DOCTOR	Orestes, / that's not
ORESTES	All we have is *this.* Just people and their outsides like shells, hard and shiny and beautiful and *hollow* – and the truth is swimming dark underneath and if you prise it out, prise truth out into the light, it evaporates as it comes to the surface.
	I don't want to answer your questions. I don't. I don't even know who you *are*.

I want this all to stop. Just *end*. This is finished.

The DOCTOR leaves ORESTES.

The grave appears, ELECTRA by it; elsewhere, KLYTEMNESTRA and AEGISTHUS are in the house.

ELECTRA   The day peels open slowly. I can't sleep but I wake – and for a moment it holds – but like a wound you forgot in the night, you move and it hits – and he's gone.

And all I can feel is that gap. The place where he should be. It doesn't close up. It's real – a solid hole engraved into the world. It feels like feeling scared.

I wish it would rain. Something at least – what's the opposite to indifferent? Different. Not the same. But it is the same. The world kept going. White clay sky. Flat land.

'In loving memory' 'In a better place' 'Sleep well' – *sleep well?* 'We will remember you always'. We. There really is no 'we'. 'Rest in peace'. You don't mean it, you don't mean anything because it isn't rest or peace – and you aren't 'we' if you're written by a single person – and it's just words. Words are defined by other words. Chasing each other round in circles until they quietly just stop existing.

And why flowers? Once it was *personal,* someone who loved flowers and this was for them – and now it's repetition, one size fits all, bled dry of all the things it used to hold, *things we do* for a reason that no one remembers.

Like the ceremony. Natural causes. Very sad. Except it *wasn't*. People nodding and saying things that might have sounded profound if you didn't speak the language – but everything had just gone – soft. Even the food.

And the flowers are dead and the language is dead and the stars are dead and the light is dead and everything reminds me of the loss, everything points to the fact that he isn't *here,* he isn't here, he isn't *here.* He survived a war. And he came home. And she –

,

The sum total of someone you knew – and it's this

Old meat buried in the earth

KLYTEMNESTRA and AEGISTHUS.

KLYTEMNESTRA	You were so much more interesting the way I imagined you.
	I couldn't stop thinking about you. I couldn't stop. Your face was everywhere and it was all the clichés, it hurt but it was a pleasure, it stretched from my throat down into my stomach and I made another person inside you.
	And it wasn't you at all.
	Was it? Was it? *Aegisthus.*
AEGISTHUS	I don't know. I can't see inside your head.
KLYTEMNESTRA	*Exactly.*
	,
AEGISTHUS	I wish we could leave the house. It's been long enough now, surely, that we can assume / that nothing …
KLYTEMNESTRA	Don't say it. Don't *say* it. Have you been drinking?

89

It's the chase isn't it. That first time. You
knew I was married. You knew who he was.
You wanted it to happen and you didn't
think it could happen so you wanted it more.
And I wanted it to happen and I thought be
brave I'll do it I'll cut the cord and just run

AEGISTHUS   I still / want it …

KLYTEMNESTRA   Two chemicals reacting. Thrown together
with such energy and then – you don't
feel it – but it's over. All that pressure and
anticipation and then in the moment you
grasp it in your arms, instead of muscle it's
just sand

I feel like I'm just waiting to die. I feel a
thousand years old.

Fuck me or something.

AEGISTHUS   It's all right for there to be quiet. It doesn't
have to be all of it all the time.

KLYTEMNESTRA screams.

ELECTRA   *Dad* I don't know what to *do*

How do you mourn? There's nothing to say.
No *response.*

I suppose this will reach you at least, mix in
with you, somewhere. And you liked wine.

*ELECTRA uncorks a bottle of red wine very easily, kisses it,
pours it into the grave. Simultaneously, AEGISTHUS turns on
the bath taps – and elsewhere, KLYTEMNESTRA pours herself
wine. The sound of water.*

KLYTEMNESTRA   I felt so alive once I'd killed him, *conscious*
that holding death in your hands is as alive
as you can ever feel – I was *free*, it was
finished. And then it slowly ran into the
ground. It's like virginity; you're a whole
new person afterwards – and you can't get
back to before. It's already gone.

CILISSA arrives to ELECTRA.

ELECTRA	Don't feel like you have to sit there in silence. I'm not my mum.
CILISSA	I can see how angry you are, Orestes.
ELECTRA	I'm not Orestes either. And anger is a natural response to an unnatural fucking act. I don't know how you can live with it. What she did.
CILISSA	She sent these flowers. Orestes, your mother / sent
ELECTRA	I'm not even going to [answer] – and my mother wouldn't send flowers – oh. You're right. That's her – her writing –

EXHIBIT: SMALL MESSAGE CARD, SEALED

ELECTRA reads the card. Doesn't read it out.

	Guilty. Maybe she'll kill herself now rather than just talking about it. I don't know why you stay with her.
CILISSA	I'm too old to leave now. Have you thought about god?
ELECTRA	I have thought about why he's not preparing a flood of vengeance to burn them both away.
CILISSA	Maybe he is.
ELECTRA	*Maybe* he's doing all sorts of things.
	Some ghost or man or judge or gods. To put things right.
	Come on then. Now. Strike her down.
	,
CILISSA	There's something – on the grave. There.

EXHIBIT: LOCK OF BROWN HAIR

ELECTRA	This? Oh. That's strange.
CILISSA	What is it?

ELECTRA	It's – someone's cut a lock of their hair and put it here
CILISSA	I don't understand. Why would you / do that?
ELECTRA	It looks like … it's exactly like …
	,
	Oh my stomach just turned to ice
CILISSA	What?
ELECTRA	My hair. It's exactly like my hair.
CILISSA	Is it your mother's?
ELECTRA	She's never been here. It's *my hair*. Is my hair falling out? And those footprints – I haven't – they're my footprints. I can even see the tendons. A perfect fit with mine. I'm mad. I haven't slept.
CILISSA	Orestes, / I think we should [go home]
ELECTRA	Orestes – yes. Of course. Orestes. It's his hair, his feet – but that means he's been here.

ORESTES is next to ELECTRA.

ORESTES:	I am here, next to you. Don't be scared, it's all right.
ELECTRA:	Is this a trap?
ORESTES:	It's Orestes. Why would I do that? The net would catch me too.
	You look –
ELECTRA:	I know. I look different now. People keep saying I look like you. Including her, but she's – it doesn't matter. Are you all right? I'm glad you're back. You left traces. The footprints. Same as mine. The hair. Same as mine.-
ORESTES:	Electra, why are you here?

ELECTRA:	She's moved him in. Aegisthus. Our new father.
ORESTES:	I know. I know.
ELECTRA:	I miss him. It's *strange* without him here. I smelled his clothes for a while but that stopped working. They're there, she hasn't burned them or anything.
	I imagine him and the sheer, sharp, *size* of how *gone* he is –
	I can't –
	I *hate* her
	,
ORESTES:	What do we do?
ELECTRA:	Nothing. There's nothing to do. Sorry. I know I'm supposed to know, and tell you how to [cope] –
	Maybe you take the damage into yourself, recovery by incorporation - except you don't recover, you re-wind yourself around the wound, you become a new thing – except I can't. And she can't.
	Always one of us waking up screaming.

KLYTEMNESTRA wakes up suddenly.

ELECTRA:	*(Chorus.)* Bad dreams.
AEGISTHUS:	*(Chorus.)* Bad dreams.
AEGISTHUS:	You were dreaming. I let you sleep. Sorry.
KLYTEMNESTRA:	The water?
AEGISTHUS:	It's just the bath.
KLYTEMNESTRA:	Agamemnon?
AEGISTHUS:	You're cold.
KLYTEMNESTRA:	Aegisthus. Don't [touch me] –

I was I was giving birth. Nurses, starch, warm water – it didn't – it didn't hurt, but then the baby, its head smelled right – and I looked and it was a snake. But I – I loved it. And I wrapped it in a cloth, a warm, comfy old cloth, full of holes, tighter, and it was hungry so I gave it my breast – and it was biting through the cloth, but then breastfeeding happily and I was *laughing* but then it started to tear the flesh, its teeth, bitter little teeth, they cut in and the blood mixed with the milk and it's hot, fluid running down me, it doesn't let go, it doesn't let go – and it *hurts*, the pain through the soft skin was – god, I want to nurse it, but I can't make it / stop –

ELECTRA: Stop. Wait. Her dream. Tell me you / see

ORESTES: See the meaning - yes

ELECTRA: It's you: the snake.

ORESTES: Or you.

ELECTRA: Same thing. It's a sign. The thing we have to do.

ORESTES: Do you believe in that?

ELECTRA: Do you remember / Iphigenia?

ORESTES: Iphigenia. No – partly -

ELECTRA: She died a long time ago, she was younger than you. But it was a sign: she died so we could win the war. And we did.-

And he died in water – just / like he said.

ORESTES: Like he said

ELECTRA: And for me, you're all that's left now. Father, sister - mother –

And what happened to him – I don't understand the point of anything if we don't

do something *against* that act, against *her,*
because *mourning* just slides off the back of it

Orestes. You know what has to happen.
What we have to do.

ELECTRA: *(Chorus.)* You don't need me to tell you

ORESTES: *(Chorus.)* I don't need you to tell me. We kill
her. We go back home. And we kill her. It's
the only thing left.

ELECTRA: Orestes, we're the same, you and me. We're
like corks - holding the net afloat - keeping it
from sinking to the depths. Hold my hand.

Dad. We hold hands.

ORESTES: Agamemnon. Dad. God or father or dad or
whichever word you'd prefer us to say – if
you can hear us. Even if you can't.

We burn this moment into the timeline.

We bear witness together that she deserves
to die, that she *has* to die, and by this hand,
this right hand – justice will shatter through
the doors and tear into her body like rotten
meat, pull her apart for what she did to you -
she has to *die,* suffer and die, she has to suffer
and learn that what she did was *wrong*

ELECTRA: We kill her like she killed you. In secret. No
sign. She has to die – or none of it makes
sense

*KLYTEMNESTRA in the bathroom. IPHIGENIA present singing
her song.*

KLYTEMNESTRA: STOP IT - STOP

She regains herself.

I am a person. I am *alive.* I could live another
fifty years. Things will improve and *grow.*
And it will come together.

The sound of wind. The feel of evening.

95

ORESTES:	It's cold. Does the disguise work?
ELECTRA:	She won't recognize you.
ORESTES:	Does the disguise work?
ELECTRA:	Yes.
ORESTES:	This house. My entire life was here. All the time bottled up inside these walls.
ELECTRA:	I'm still here too - Orestes, do you love me?
ORESTES:	I think I need you outside.
KLYTEMNESTRA:	I'd like to hear some music.

,

ORESTES	Hello? Hello?
CILISSA	Who is it?
ORESTES	I'm not a threat. We're travelling alone. I've got something to say to the lady of the house.
CILISSA	To say? Who are you?
ORESTES	Look can you either let me in or send a man out or something because I haven't got *time.* Send me a man and at least I can have a straightforward conversation.

ORESTES enters the house. Same position as AGAMEMNON was twice before.

I'm home.

KLYTEMNESTRA enters, surprised anyone is present in the house.

KLYTEMNESTRA	Good evening.
ORESTES	Good evening. You might want to sit down

She works it out fast.

KLYTEMNESTRA	Oh – I dreamed this once. Orestes. He's dead. Isn't he? Dead.

ORESTES	I'm not the official [message, but] – yes. Orestes is dead. I'm sorry, I don't know more than that, but I know that's [right]
KLYTEMNESTRA	right. Yes. Well, thank you for, uh –

,

I hate this house. There's no escape.
I thought he was finally gone, I hoped he'd
– but hope is a lie, you realise, it's the feeling you can ever really win.

He's dead, you're *sure* he's dead?

Sorry, yes, I'm in shock, probably.

You must have come a long way. Please stay here, rest tonight –

CILISSA	I nursed him at my breast. He drank my milk.
KLYTEMNESTRA	Yes.
CILISSA	Sickly baby, he was. He screamed and screamed at night. Never a good sleeper.
KLYTEMNESTRA	Yes.
CILISSA	Babies are little animals; never can tell whether they're hungry or thirsty or what – their insides are a law unto themselves. I used to always read him wrong, you'd wind him and then he'd mess himself, '*that's* what you were crying at', constantly washing his clothes – nurse, cleaner, and – I just can't believe it. I wore away my life for him.

How old was he? It's really no age at all.
There's no justice.

KLYTEMNESTRA	She'll find you somewhere clean to sleep.
ORESTES	Yes. Thank you. I really am sorry.
KLYTEMNESTRA	There's several storeys of rooms. There are clean towels and please just help yourself to

anything you need. Or want. There's wine. If you'd like a hot bath or anything. That's fine. I think I'll go to sleep.

KLYTEMNESTRA exits.

CILISSA Excuse me, I wouldn't trust her. Her eyes are always hiding something. I don't trust them. I'm just saying, I don't know you, but be careful what you say in this house. There's always been unhappiness here. He was a good little boy. Quiet. Thoughtful. There's no justice.

Thank you for coming back.

ORESTES moves to the bathroom. His father's dressing gown is there, the red one. He puts it on. It's too big. He puts his hand in the pocket and there's a crumpled up note. He reads it: the text reads CHILD KILLER. He sneezes. He turns and AGAMEMNON is watching him. Their eyes meet.

KLYTEMNESTRA Aegisthus? Darling?

ORESTES Agamemnon. It's a sign, isn't it? An instruction. Received. Thank you.

ORESTES runs to him, hugs him. As they separate from the hug, blood everywhere, all over both of them.

KLYTEMNESTRA Aegisthus? Aegisthus, what's going on?

AEGISTHUS. TIME OF DEATH: [[TODAY'S DATE, THE TIME]].

CILISSA rushes in panicked.

CILISSA He's alive, he's – the dead are killing the living –

KLYTEMNESTRA He?

She works it out.

That story wasn't a – it was a plot. OK, you need to move now and get me a weapon –

MOVE woman, don't just –

Enter ORESTES. *He makes for her and she moves swiftly, talking all the time: her words are the only weapon she has.*

ORESTES — Mum. I'm here to make things right.

KLYTEMNESTRA — Orestes. Thank you for coming back. Thank you.

I know why you've come. But it's more complicated than you think, and you need to listen –

'

Your father was a killer, and it's my fault, it's my fault who I chose to mate with but you do not want to become your father

ORESTES — I am him. I'm half him. Look at – he's me, he's / *me*

AEGISTHUS *is covered in blood. He sits down at the table and becomes* AGAMEMNON.

KLYTEMNESTRA — And *so am I.* He killed your sister, he killed my daughter, and she isn't here any more. She isn't here any more. I know you think this this comes from your instinct, or from – some – I don't know – heroic idea of what a son does but your father has a hook sunk into your soul, and, without you even knowing, is pulling you back towards him. I know you grew up with it – I'm not saying it's your fault, it's not your fault, but you don't want to *be him, you do not want blood on your hands.* That's just not you – and this isn't how it ends for us, there's so much more – we grow old together, Orestes, me and you. I'm your mum.

ORESTES *runs to his mother and hugs her.*

It's all right. Nothing has happened. Let's go back.

ORESTES   Yes.

KLYTEMNESTRA   Orestes. Orestes. Orestes.

He relaxes. Things slightly clear. Then she rings the dinner bell. She laughs from exhaustion. For the final time, dinner is laid. It's slow. There's just two of them now. Occasional bangings from outside, wind blowing. Suspended. Held. Uncertain.

KLYTEMNESTRA   Eat something. You must be hungry. It should be meat really, I'm sorry, but I can't seem to face it these days –

ORESTES opens the wine. KLYTEMNESTRA laughs – notices.

ORESTES   Where's Electra?

KLYTEMNESTRA   What, darling?

ORESTES looks at his mother. He realises:

ORESTES   *(Chorus.)* Something's wrong
KLYTEMNESTRA   *(Chorus.)* Something's wrong

Enter ELECTRA, suddenly, late

ELECTRA   If you're not here, you don't eat

Blackout of only a few seconds. When the lights come up, ELECTRA is struggling with KLYTEMNESTRA – both over the top of each other, screaming:

ELECTRA   You destroyed our home – you killed my dad. You're not my home, no mother would / be able to – How could you do it to us – he was the only thing that held it together – and you sacrificed all of that and us and him, and now you're here, sitting in everything he created, with some man in his bed, wearing his clothes, and god I want you to DIE I HATE YOU

KLYTEMNESTRA   I did the *right thing*

Blackout of another few seconds. When the lights come up, ORESTES is exactly where ELECTRA was – and ELECTRA has vanished.

KLYTEMNESTRA	If you kill me, you kill yourself / Orestes
ORESTES	You did wrong. Now you suffer wrong.
KLYTEMNESTRA	I know what's right for you. I am your *mother.*

KLYTEMNESTRA unexpectedly bares her breast

| | I fed both of you from this breast, inside me, Iphigenia – and you. You were given *life* |

,

ORESTES	This is / your dream.
KLYTEMNESTRA	That dream. The snake was you.
DOCTOR	Orestes. What happened?
ORESTES	My sister with me – she kills my – mother –

IPHIGENIA on stage somehow.

| DOCTOR | Orestes. Listen. Your sister died. Your sister died. Orestes? Let's please just try and reconnect with that. |

ORESTES' nose is bleeding.

ORESTES	No, that's not her – that's – it was Electra, she kills her –
DOCTOR	Electra?
ORESTES	Yes
DOCTOR	Where was Electra?
ORESTES	She was outside – no, inside, at the table, in the house …
DOCTOR	And where were you?

The DOCTOR becomes more insistent, firmer.

| | Whose hair did you find at the grave? |
| ORESTES | Mine. No. *She* found it. The lock of – that's how she knew it was me – |

DOCTOR	Your hair was the same? And your footprints and hers were the same? A girl? That doesn't make sense. Listen to me. Orestes.
ORESTES	No: Electra was there: we were there together –
DOCTOR	I think we have to consider the possibility that those were *your* footprints, that that was *your* hair –
ORESTES	I feel like my head has split in two, it keeps *shifting* but Electra
DOCTOR	Orestes. I don't know who that is.
	You've survived a trauma. Your sister died, Orestes: your sister, Iphigenia. She died. You survived. We have no record of another sister. You had *one* sister.
	What are you holding?

ORESTES looks at his hands. There's a sudden blackout. Then lights up and KLYTEMNESTRA's dead, sprawled across the table. ORESTES holds his hands out – they're bloodied. Perhaps he wears a saffron dress. A sense of dawning calm.

ORESTES	This was always going to happen.
	She's been dead since the beginning.

KLYTEMNESTRA. TIME OF DEATH: [[TODAY'S DATE, THE TIME]].

DOCTOR	So you're alone?
ORESTES	yes
DOCTOR	And you killed her? What are you holding?

CILISSA has entered, stands, looking at the pool of blood. Somehow she's in the shade. Something is slightly different about her.

ORESTES	I feel like we're travelling fast, I've gone off road and I don't know where I'm heading and I'm – my heart is racing – but I ended it, it's – look at this, this cloth, destroyed,

destroyed like the family, the house
destroyed by her, I don't know what to call
it, a tablecloth, a flag, a net, a trap, a curtain
for a bath, a snare – a shroud – it was a
perfect thing and she threw it across my
father's eyes and stabbed it full of holes – to
this. There's *nothing* good here but – she had
to *die,* suffer and *learn* and die. And now it's
done.

EXHIBIT: TORN AND BLOODSTAINED CLOTH

He throws the thing over his mother like a shroud. The
DOCTOR is wearing court robes, she seems different, suddenly:

DOCTOR	Could we have the next exhibit? Thank you.
ORESTES	What did you say? I don't –
DOCTOR	We need to reconstruct your act. We need to be sure.
DOCTOR FURY	*(Chorus.)* What are you holding? *(Chorus.)* What are you holding?
FURY	It won't wash away. It stains. This is who you are now.
DOCTOR	Orestes. Answer the question. What are you holding?

The actor who played CILISSA has become the Fury. She is
terrifying, inhuman. Perhaps she holds a real snake.

Other people start to enter – ORESTES feels he is going mad.
He could be right; or we could be, for the first time, seeing
things as they really are.

FURY	Your father killed the girl. So your mother killed *him.* And you killed *her.* Now she must be avenged. There is a death outstanding. The child is the price.
ORESTES	Who are you?
DOCTOR	Who? Orestes – who?
FURY	There is a death outstanding.

ORESTES   The – *fury,* her – there's something wrong. Is this a dream?

DOCTOR   Orestes, you're seeing things and that is concomitant with serious mental illness. Madness. I understand that this is difficult but I need you to answer the question. What are you holding?

To his surprise, ORESTES' *hands are suddenly handcuffed.*

Something big happens to the feel of the space, something formal, huge: electric, shadowy, smooth. The light on ORESTES *gets whiter and whiter.*

FURY   I am only what you feel. And the water breaks through the walls, the blood breaks out of the vein, and the runner slips with a relentless doom. You cannot know you fall – and a mist descends over the house, white foam sprouting out, cursed, infected

ORESTES   I need you to help me. You're here to help me

DOCTOR   No. We're here to try and understand the truth. What are you holding?

Trolleys of papers. Each of the exhibits is displayed somewhere, behind glass. Everyone wears robes oddly reminiscent of Agamemnon's dressing gown. The flavour of a court, wooden tables, microphones. ATHENE *sits as judge – she is played by the actor who played Cassandra. A crest of two eagles killing a hare. The doctor now seems to be a lawyer (but we'll call her* DOCTOR *still, simply for ease of playing).* CALCHAS *takes an official role in proceedings, a kind of clerk of court.*

The stage is now a dream-like version of a court – at once familiar and strange. Everyone is waiting for ORESTES *to speak.*

ATHENE   The respondent must *answer the question.*

AGAMEMNON	My lady, could we request that the question is repeated?
DOCTOR	What are you holding?
ORESTES	It's right – bright – silver – a knife – a knife

CALCHAS puts it finally in his hand.

EXHIBIT: SILVER KNIFE, BLOODSTAINED

DOCTOR	And you confess that you killed your mother?

,

ORESTES	Yes
DOCTOR	Thank you, my lady. No further questions.
AGAMEMNON	Can I therefore request a break, my lady / given that
ATHENE	Granted.
CALCHAS	Please be upstanding.

Everyone stands. ATHENE leaves.

We pause there. Thank you.

The act is over.

ACT FOUR

Throughout the pause, the company reassemble. They wear court robes. They are simultaneously the characters they have already played this evening, and representatives in the court case. The FURY is present.

ORESTES	Where are we?
CALCHAS	What do you mean?

KLYTEMNESTRA enters.

ORESTES	Is that / my mother?
CALCHAS	Your mother's representative.
ORESTES	Who are all the people?
CALCHAS	They're here for you.

ORESTES notices that one of the walls has partly fallen in. In fact, the room itself is crumbling, as if the set itself has aged in the course of the evening.

ORESTES	It feels familiar. It feels like I've always been here.
DOCTOR	That's hardly surprising.

Something crumbles above and a little dust falls.

ORESTES	It's falling apart.
AGAMEMNON	We don't talk like that here.
CALCHAS	Please be upstanding.

ATHENE enters.

ATHENE	Thank you for coming back. Thank you.

People sit down.

I would remind this house that it must consider every step of the evidence presented, as it bears witness to each story, each committed act and makes its judgment. It must consider what it does not know:

the gaps in the available evidence. It is
incumbent on this house as a collective that
the care taken in this case is no less than if
you yourself were the respondent.

ORESTES   Is this a dream? Am I / mad?

CALCHAS   The respondent should please observe the
times to speak and to be silent.

ATHENE   We have now witnessed completed re-
enactments at – could we clarify – [amass the
evidence]?

Folders, boxes are brought in, piled on tables.

CALCHAS   Each actor of each respective action here
is guilty of murder – though only the
respondent lives to undergo examination.
The first act the killing of the child,
Iphigenia, at [[TIME OF DEATH]], the
second act the killing of the husband
Agamemnon by his wife at [[TIME OF
DEATH]], and the examination and
enactment of the third act concluded
before the break - the killing of the mother
Klytemnestra at the hands of the respondent
at [[TIME OF DEATH]]. The respondent
has confessed to the third act.

ATHENE   Are there immediate objections arising from
any of the prior exhibits? Anything further to
submit?

AGAMEMNON and KLYTEMNESTRA both shake their heads.

Then: we present conclusions and we move
to judgement

CALCHAS   Please be upstanding. This house now moves
to judgement.

ATHENE   As the embodiment of both heaven and
earth, state and god, male and female,
I announce myself the higher power of

right, and I inaugurate this house once again for our purpose as a house of *justice* with mandate to establish, enforce and engender what is right.

Everyone acknowledges.

CALCHAS   Please raise your hands and answer the questions.

ATHENE   Do you submit to the practice of this house?

ORESTES   I don't think I believe / in

CALCHAS   This is not a religious house.

ORESTES   And – why swear if it isn't a / religious

AGAMEMNON   We don't talk like that here.

CALCHAS   The respondent should observe the times to speak and to be silent.

ATHENE   My role here is to *represent* the gods.

ORESTES raises his hands.

Do you submit to the practice of this house?

ORESTES   – the practice of this house? What / is this?

The FURY laughs.

FURY   There is a death outstanding. The child is the price.

ORESTES   What is the practice of this house? What are you going to do?

Some conferring.

CALCHAS   The respondent has a right to make the request.

ATHENE   Very well. Orestes, you killed your mother. This house will proceed to consider your act. We hear both sides. We make a judgement.

ORESTES   Judgement?

ATHENE	In the absence of a living family member to avenge your victim, this house and its systems inherit your judgement collectively.
	Do you submit to the / practice of –
ORESTES	The penalty is death. The judgement. If I'm not set free, you're going to kill me. At the end. That's what happens, isn't it?
ATHENE	Yes. Your life for your mother's.
CALCHAS	Could we please keep to procedure?
ATHENE	Do you submit to the practice of this house?
ORESTES	I do
CALCHAS	Please read the lines in front of you.
ORESTES	I swear to tell the truth – the whole truth – a true and binding version of events –
	,
	in the sight of – ?
CALCHAS	Theous.
	Zeus. Allah. El. Jehovah. Janus. Jupiter. Jove. Elah. 'ilah. Elohim. Ishvara. Ra. Raven. Dagda. Anguta. Yahweh. Apollo. Olorun. Chronus. Osiris. Brahman. Buddah. Odin. The Mountain. The Godhead. The Way. The Door. The Truth. The Life. The Light. The Lamb. The Creator. The Maker. The Supreme Being. The Holy Name. The One. The King. The Lord. The Judge. The Father. The All-Knowing, who can never be known.
	God. Gods. Instinct. Primal fluids that sense the future.
ORESTES	I swear to tell the truth – I can't swear. I don't / know

AGAMEMNON	Forgive me, my lady – Orestes. We are trying to reconstruct your story, the events, what happ/ened
ORESTES	But some things *happen*. How can / I swear to tell the truth?
ATHENE	Could we *please* keep to procedure?
AGAMEMNON	Orestes, as best you can, you swear to give the true version / of what you did
ORESTES	There *isn't* one true version. There isn't. There isn't one story – a line of truth that stretches start to end. That doesn't happen any more, maybe it never happened, but even as I say this now, as I say *this* now, in each of your minds you create your own versions, different lenses pointing at the same thing at the same time and *seeing that thing differently* – it depends on too much – the day you've had, what you feel about *your* mother, the thought you thought before this one – it all floods in, this thing this whole thing is *helpless* because your brain creates stories in which it is *right*

The FURY *laughs.*

ATHENE	Do you refuse to swear to tell the truth?
DOCTOR	My lady / this is unacceptable
TALTHYBIUS	My lady, one moment. Orestes, do you believe you were wrong to kill your mother? The story your brain told you, was it
ORESTES	I –
TALTHYBIUS	Was it the right thing?
ORESTES	Yes
TALTHYBIUS	Then will you undertake to persuade this house of that? This house exists to enact justice and justice will be done

Something else happens to the house: something crumbles somewhere.

ORESTES   How long have I been here? How long has /
               this been

ATHENE   You undertake to tell the truth, to tell here
               today a true and binding version of events?

               ,

ORESTES   Yes.

               To KLYTEMNESTRA:

ATHENE   The representative may continue

               The FURY *laughs, low and slow.*

KLYTEMNESTRA   Thank you, my lady. Resuming with
               some final questions before proceeding to
               conclusion.

ATHENE   Thank you.

DOCTOR   We heard before that you killed your mother.
               Is that correct? / Try to be clear.

AGAMEMNON   This has already been established, my lady.

ORESTES   Yes

DOCTOR   How did you kill her?

ORESTES   A knife.

DOCTOR   I couldn't hear / that, I'm afraid.

ORESTES   With a knife.

DOCTOR   Why?

MENELAUS   In vengeance for his father. On instruction of
               the gods, my lady.

ATHENE   For the last time, let the respondent answer
               the questions.

DOCTOR   Thank you, my lady. Orestes, the gods spoke
               to you?

ORESTES   Yes.

DOCTOR	Directly?
ORESTES	There were signs
DOCTOR	So not directly. Were there not similar signs endorsing the first act, read by your father as sanctioning his murder of your sister, his daughter?
AGAMEMNON	The respondent does not remember, he was too young, we have been through this / already, my lady
ATHENE	The respondent must answer the question.
ORESTES	There were signs then, I think. And he read them correctly.
KLYTEMNESTRA	I'm sorry – how do you know?
ORESTES	The wind came. They won the war.
KLYTEMNESTRA	Can we prove that Iphigenia's death caused those events? Do we *know* it would not have happened anyway?
	,
ORESTES	No.
DOCTOR	Could you tell us what the signs were that night, the night of your mother's / murder?
AGAMEMNON	My lady, we have already witnessed / this reconstructed in its –
ATHENE	Continue.
ORESTES	I went back to his house in disguise, I was, in the room in which my father died, and in his pocket, I found a note, it said 'CHILD KILLER'.
CALCHAS	Submitting to the house the exhibit.

EXHIBIT: HANDWRITTEN NOTE, WITH ENVELOPE

ORESTES	It was a sign from him, beyond the grave – or from god. I was his child, I was to be his avenger, the killer / on the –
KLYTEMNESTRA	I'm sorry – why does it have to be only one thing? Can it not be more?
	Could it not have been a note sent to your father by one of the many people who disagreed, passionately disagreed, with military action which resulted in the deaths of countless innocent children? Was he too – in several senses – not a *child killer*? Might the note have been penned by his wife?
MENELAUS	It is some coincidence for this not to be meaningful: the will of the gods / is clear –
KLYTEMNESTRA	My lady, could we clarify – how the gods / might
ATHENE	Gods speak in signs. Signs are interpretable. Open.

Something else crumbles, gently sets alight. Only ORESTES *registers.*

DOCTOR	If we might travel back along the road, all the way back to where things began – the exhibit, thank you –

The drawing from the very beginning is put into ORESTES' *hands.*

EXHIBIT: DRAWING OF HARE KILLED BY TWO EAGLES

A pregnant mother hare, killed by two eagles.

ORESTES	It's the death of Iphigenia, of my sister. The eagles are my father and his brother, the mother hare is my mother – and Iphigenia dies in the womb. She didn't know.
DOCTOR	But – I'm sorry – the mother also dies. Could we not submit that the death of the mother hare is the death of your mother

ORESTES	And the eagles are me and – yes. It could be that.
DOCTOR	She's been dead since the beginning.
MENELAUS	My lady, what point / is being made here?
KLYTEMNESTRA	Or could we offer this interpretation: the eagles are simply the symbol of this house. The eagles represent justice, and the pregnant hare is the respondent.
AGAMEMNON	My lady, this is / just not appropriate
KLYTEMNESTRA	The pregnant hare is the respondent – and the children are his children set free from having ever to be born – when he is executed by this house
AGAMEMNON	My lady, this is / unacceptable
ATHENE	State your case
KLYTEMNESTRA	We read the signs like mirrors, my lady. They show us what we want and nothing more.
FURY	There is a death outstanding.
KLYTEMNESTRA	What injuries did your mother suffer at your hands?
	,
ORESTES	I killed her, I don't remember / what her injuries were
AGAMEMNON	My lady, this is unacceptable
KLYTEMNESTRA	Perhaps if we travel further backwards. How did you gain access to your mother's house?
ORESTES	In disguise.
KLYTEMNESTRA	In disguise. So you had already decided on your course of action? You knew what you were there to do.
ORESTES	Yes.

KLYTEMNESTRA   Some part of you must recognize that,
if you had to keep it secret, then *maybe* it was
wrong?

ORESTES   Yes. I recognize [that] – but she killed my /
father.

KLYTEMNESTRA   What did your mother say as you raised your
knife?

AGAMEMNON   She *was a murderer herself.* My lady, we have
already witnessed / what happened

KLYTEMNESTRA   What did your mother / say?

MENELAUS   My lady, there is no need to make him say
the words / he has confessed –

ATHENE   This house must hear all of the evidence,
all of the competing versions, and make its
judgement then. Continue.

KLYTEMNESTRA   What did your mother say?

What did *she say*?

Then let us witness it again. Could you?
And – thank you – [read it –]

CALCHAS   'I know what's right for you. I am your
mother. I fed both of you from this breast,
inside me, Iphigenia and you, you were
given *life.*' There is then a silence of several
seconds.

ORESTES   This is / your dream.

KLYTEMNESTRA   That dream. The snake was you.

,

And you hesitated?

ORESTES   Yes.

KLYTEMNESTRA   Why?

,

	You looked into your mother's eyes and hesitated – I imagine she was scared. She knew. And part of you was unsure what to do. That's right, isn't it?
ORESTES	How can we ever be sure. Of any decision about any thing.

,

KLYTEMNESTRA	Of course you couldn't be sure. Of course. This was your mother. Your hesitation is a recorded fact. And what that hesitation represents is a screaming acknowledgement that murder is wrong, that the murder of a mother is a crime which even then, at that moment, you knew was wrong, acceptable in no code or system or law – no social law, even the law of nature. Against the fact of your birth. Your blood. She was your mother. You knew it was wrong.
ORESTES	Yes. Yes. You're right. That's right. I did love / her.
KLYTEMNESTRA	Thank you
ORESTES	I'm sorry – I'm sorry
FURY	There is a death outstanding.
AGAMEMNON	My lady, if I may – Orestes, where were you?
ORESTES	Here. Right here.
AGAMEMNON	And when did you take that step forward – towards her? Where were you when you killed her?
ORESTES	I … I don't remember
AGAMEMNON	Could you repeat that, please?
ORESTES	I don't remember

AGAMEMNON	My lady, the last memory the respondent has is of the hesitation – and all that hesitation represents is a gap in the evidence we have. The respondent has suffered the loss of his father, of his sister, we saw, even in this house, how deeply those traumas have affected him, how the balance of his mind / was under constant attack
DOCTOR	This was a pre-meditated attack carried out in disguise: hardly the actions of a madman, hardly someone in mental distress –
AGAMEMNON	He has spoken about his deceased sister in / this house
KLYTEMNESTRA	His madness is still his, it is still *him*. We cannot discount *parts* of the respondent's personality, either he is responsible for his actions, or he is not.
AGAMEMNON	There is a history here: his mother had herself attempted suicide
ORESTES	That wasn't / true, she said things –
DOCTOR	We can *not* admit *your* story and not the story of your victim.
MENELAUS	What part of the victim's story do we in fact possess?
ATHENE	Could we please keep to procedure?

The FURY is banging on the table.

ORESTES	She paid NO PRICE. Nothing *happened* to her, she didn't suffer for what she'd done / she *meant* it, she was *sure*
TALTHYBIUS	*(Chorus.)* My lady, the respondent is under extreme pressure and a line of questioning which is frankly irrelevant
DOCTOR	*(Chorus.)* How could you possibly know that?
ATHENE	Could we please keep to procedure?

DOCTOR	Moreover, her act was not like yours. Agamemnon did not lift her from her crib. He did not breastfeed her.
ORESTES	But that's *different* / it's not a –
KLYTEMNESTRA	Everything always is. All families are different, my lady, and yet always exactly the same. We are hurt, so we hurt back. Agamemnon had murdered his daughter. And for that first act / Klytemnestra *rightly* sought revenge
AGAMEMNON	His act served the greatest possible good – he sacrificed his family for the state. My lady, he had fought and won a war: he was safe, he thought, from death. He was *in his bath* – can we see the [evidence] – when she *struck*, covered his eyes with this cloth, blinded him and cut him to pieces

EXHIBIT: TORN AND BLOODSTAINED CLOTH

MENELAUS	He only killed his daughter for our good. And his murder was an act that tore at the fabric of this country's security, it hurt us / all
KLYTEMNESTRA	And she *paid* for that act with her life. Once the blood has soaked into the carpet it can't flow back into the body: that woman who killed him is dead.
FURY	The child is the price.
ATHENE	Could we please keep to procedure? Are we any closer to conclusion?
KLYTEMNESTRA	Thank you, my lady. What injuries did your mother suffer at your hands?
AGAMEMNON	The respondent has been clear that he / does not remember
KLYTEMNESTRA	We have not witnessed what he did. We might at least exhibit how *she* died. Could we please [read the report]?

AGAMEMNON	This is / completely unnecessary
KLYTEMNESTRA	THIS IS THE STORY. THESE ARE THE FACTS. Thank you.
CALCHAS	'Time of death [[22:12]]. The body is that of a [[well-developed, well-nourished Caucasian]] female which weighs [[129 pounds]] and measures [[65 inches]] from crown to sole. Both upper and lower teeth are natural, without evidence of injury to the cheeks, lips or gums.'
KLYTEMNESTRA	You can take a step forward here –
AGAMEMNON	These facts are not material to the decision before this house
KLYTEMNESTRA	My lady, my equivalent seems not to have understood that we have only one unquestionable fact. That fact is Klytemnestra's corpse. Cold and hard. And real. Her carcass is the *only* fact. It proves two things: the existence of her killer, and the way in which she died. These are then the material facts before we move to conclude. Continue. Please / continue
CALCHAS	'At the time of autopsy examination, rigor mortis has set in. The body is not embalmed. Bruising of the limbs, especially of the hands and feet, strongly suggests struggle. There are very numerous incised and stab wounds of the neck, torso and genitals, which will below be itemised. These sharp force injuries ultimately led to transection of the left and right common carotid arteries, as well as incisions of the left and right internal jugular veins which in turn caused fatal exsanguinating haemorrhage'
ORESTES	Each thing leading to the next thing

ORESTES is sobbing

MENELAUS   My lady the respondent is becoming
                  extremely distressed / this is distressing in
                  the extreme

KLYTEMNESTRA   As he himself best knows, this is what
                  happened / to her.

MENELAUS   My lady, there is no need for / this to
                  continue

KLYTEMNESTRA   *This is what he did*, these are the
                  consequences OF HIS OWN ACTIONS my
                  lady

ATHENE   Continue

CALCHAS   'The primary deep incised wound of the
                  neck is gaping and exposes the larynx and
                  cervical vertebral column. It measures four
                  and a half by three inches in length and is
                  found diagonally oriented at the level of the
                  superior border of the larynx. On the ...'
                  some text has been lost here ... 'upwardly
                  angulated toward the right earlobe. On
                  the left side it is transversely oriented and
                  extends three inches to the anterior border
                  of the left sternocleidomastoid muscle.'
                  There are gaps in the text here too, my
                  lady, picking up ... 'edges of the wound
                  are smooth ... ' the text here is corrupted,
                  continuing 'intramuscular haemorrhage,
                  fresh, dark-red purple, evident'

TALTHYBIUS   My lady –

DOCTOR   There is more / my lady

TALTHYBIUS   This evidence is full of holes, my lady, we
                  have not borne witness to the event itself

DOCTOR   My lady, we submit that it is impossible for
                  this house to witness the event itself, what
                  really happened. None of us know. None of
                  us *can* know. We can only reconstruct the
                  way she died.

ATHENE	To which this house has already borne witness.
TALTHYBIUS	Thank you, my lady.
KLYTEMNESTRA	My lady, we now move to conclude.
CALCHAS	Please be upstanding. The house now moves to conclusion.
ATHENE	Thank you.
KLYTEMNESTRA	If the respondent had murdered his mother once for every reason he had, she'd have died several times – once for the gods, once for his father, once because he was not in his / right mind
ORESTES	Yes – she's / right – she's right
AGAMEMNON	Orestes
CALCHAS	The respondent should please observe the times to speak and to be silent. The representative may continue.
KLYTEMNESTRA	Thank you. A sister, a father, a mother – are dead. There has to come an end. But allow me to ask the house: why does the murder of the mother count for less than that of the father? Because the woman is less important. Why is the mother's motive for revenge *lesser* than the son's? She avenged a daughter; he a father. Because the *woman* is less important. This woman has paid the price. But this house cannot be a place where the woman is less important.
FURY	There is a death outstanding. The child is the price.
KLYTEMNESTRA	How are we to resolve the respondent's double role? He is both the surviving son of the victim – and the victim's murderer. He by right should argue both for his innocence and his guilt. He is bound to both sides of

this house. My lady, our conclusion is clear: the respondent must avenge the murder of his mother – by taking his own life.

FURY   By his hand alone. The child is the price.

,

KLYTEMNESTRA   In doing so, we submit that he will eliminate the last member of a family which has almost eliminated itself.

AGAMEMNON   My lady, we cannot *kill* the respondent *symbolically* – he is a *person* not a fact, this *house* is people, not symbols: he will still die. This house / must find

ORESTES   STOP STOP STOP / STOP

CALCHAS   The respondent must observe the times to speak and to be silent.

ATHENE   The system of this house is clear. The / representatives act on behalf of

ORESTES   You can't use some system from centuries ago to explain – there is no explaining why, she'd done what she did because of my sister, but she also had a *lover* – there are *too many things* here, what use is the system, what *use* is the system, what *justice* can it possibly perform – you can't just *decide* what I felt or why – there is no explaining *why*

ATHENE   The *representative* may continue

ORESTES   She stabbed him so hard they couldn't get the bits of cloth out of his skin / cloth hardened like a net

AGAMEMNON   The respondent has undergone a trauma and clearly presents *no further danger* to / any living person

KLYTEMNESTRA   He presented no danger before. But this house / exists for justice –

ORESTES is exhausted but this comes from somewhere deep.

ORESTES   This house is falling apart. And what *does* this *mean?* How can you punish a *natural impulse?* Who is that *for?* Who benefits? How are things BETTER? It won't stop revenge, it won't stop murder. It is still going to happen it was *always going to happen.*

ATHENE   This house is all of us. Its beliefs / are the

ORESTES   It doesn't believe. Once upon a time, someone just made it up. And in here you forget that moment before it existed. *It's just people.* That's all there *is.* And what I feel, what I felt, what I did – it could have been any of you – we can't eliminate [it] – it's us, it's it's what a person / is

ATHENE   This house is *all* of us.

             You made this happen. It came from you.

ORESTES looks at the people. His nose is bleeding.

ORESTES   I can't go on. I want to stop.

ATHENE   Is that your conclusion complete?

KLYTEMNESTRA It is, my lady.

ATHENE   I accept the submission. The respondent dies by his own hand if the house returns a guilty verdict. We will now proceed to judgement.

AGAMEMNON   My lady, could we take a moment before – ?

             ,

ATHENE   One minute.

CALCHAS   Please be upstanding. We pause there for one minute. One minute. Thank you.

Like a pause but not one – the staging language should match each of the act breaks used in the production.

AGAMEMNON   Orestes. You need to prepare for the vote.

ORESTES	A vote
AGAMEMNON	It can't be just a single person. The decision is too complex for one. It has to be more.
ORESTES	But what if someone hates me or misheard the / evidence or
AGAMEMNON	That could happen if one person decided.

,

ORESTES	But what if they do the wrong thing?
TALTHYBIUS	Then – they're all implicated in the consequences.
ORESTES	But it's madness – it doesn't change anything. I mean, because they say I'm guilty that doesn't make me *guilty*. It's not like the atoms in my body change into guilty atoms, it it – it's arbitrary. It's wrong.
AGAMEMNON	I know it's not perfect. It's an old idea, that if we all sit together in the same space and listen and consider the problem, suspend our doubt, trust that meaning will come, and we do it for long enough and we look hard enough – in the end, somehow, something will come of that.
ORESTES	It's – it's fragile.
MENELAUS	It's been like that for a long time.

MENELAUS and TALTHYBIUS leave.

ORESTES	Dad? *What's going on?*

,

AGAMEMNON	Orestes –
ORESTES	I –
AGAMEMNON	There's no more time

The pause ends.

Thank you, my lady

ATHENE	This house has witnessed the entire story. The respondent's mother and father were both murderers – he himself is the last of his house. It is undeniably complex. But the judgement before us is simple. Innocence or guilt.

The FURY laughs at ORESTES.

Let me remind you to think not of this one instance but of the instances to come, people thousands of years from today. Your judgement will judge them; the justice we serve will be their justice too.

CALCHAS addresses the audience.

CALCHAS	The respondent's life is forfeit if he is found guilty of the murder of his mother. He is freed if he is found innocent. We have borne witness to the evidence. And now this house must vote.

Think clearly of one word and hold it in your mind – either 'INNOCENT' or 'GUILTY'. Make that judgement. In 3. 2. 1.

Thank you.

ORESTES is brought forward. CALCHAS puts a tray into his hands.

What are you holding?

ORESTES	A silver tray on which are three small, pleated paper cups. One of them contains a small amount of translucent liquid. The second one contains a small orange tablet. The third one a sweet-flavoured liquid.

The child is the price.

KLYTEMNESTRA	Orestes. You won't suffer. It won't hurt.
AGAMEMNON	Home. It'll feel like coming home.

ORESTES   And the family is waiting for me.
               Everybody's there. I'm the last one, in at the
               very end.

A bell rings.

               It could have been me at the start.

ATHENE   Do we have a verdict?

CALCHAS   We do.

               My lady, I present the decision of this house
               in relation to the case of the respondent,
               Orestes, the charge of murder, his story as
               presented, and his act of matricide, to which
               he has confessed.

               The judgement of the house is binding.

               On [[DAY, the DATE^th of MONTH]] at
               precisely [[TODAY'S TIME]] this house
               found that

               Found that –

*He reads the result. For the first time, he seems not to know
what to do.*

               The vote is tied.

               My lady, there are equal votes for both sides.

               ,

ATHENE   In the case of a tied ballot I believe it falls to
               me to conclude the judgement.

ORESTES   That's – that's just one person

ATHENE   Is that correct? That it is my deciding vote?

CALCHAS   I believe that is the procedure, my lady, yes

ATHENE   If there are no objections? In the practice of
               our lives, we favour men in all things – in our
               society, in our religion, and in our law – and
               as the just representative of our society, our
               religion and our law, it is appropriate that on

behalf of this house of justice it is emphasised that men are favoured.

Judgement is as follows, which constitutes my vote, and which is based upon the presumption of innocence: on the charge of murder, this house finds the respondent not guilty – and he is therefore acquitted with immediate effect.

'

ORESTES can't speak, he's overcome.

Justice is done and the house is adjourned.

The FURY is putting on court robes. Everyone else starts to leave.

CALCHAS	The house is adjourned.
ORESTES	My lady – I don't know whether – what is *real,* whether –
	Does she belong here?
CALCHAS	We need her here. A murderer should fear the retribution of this house. A murder cannot just be wiped away. She is essential: the terror she holds keeps us from collapse. It keeps the house of justice standing. She is a part of us. And we of her.
ORESTES	But – what is she?
AGAMEMNON	What do you think she is?
ORESTES	She's – pure – *fury* …
KLYTEMNESTRA	No, she's just like us. She's *kind.*
ORESTES	It's not about the word we use –
KLYTEMNESTRA	You see, I think it is.
ORESTES	One vote and I'm dead. It's – I mean. One person. The bias. I wasn't *sure.* Yes, I am [relieved] it's just – so – *small.*

Excuse me – my mother, my father, my family, they're dead. They all die.

What happened?

CALCHAS   They find you innocent. But you already knew that.

You're free.

ORESTES   But I still killed her.

Where does it end?

,

Perhaps I always *feel* guilty

,

What do I do?

What do I do?

What do I do?

What do I do?

The act is over.